Hidden Lives

*The roots of living peace
lie deep in
creativity and joy.
To the hope of such peace,
this book is dedicated.*

Hidden Lives

Stories from the East End

by the people of
42 Balaam Street,
Plaistow

with a preface by
Benjamin Zephaniah

compiled and edited by
Deborah Padfield

© Helping Hands 1999

Published in the United Kingdom by *Eastside Community Heritage*,
Old Town Hall, Stratford, Newham, and *Curlew Productions*, Thirlestane
House, Kelso, TD5 8PD, Scotland.

Cover design by *Stan Peskett*
Map by *Robert Smart*
Photographs by *Donna Evans, Piotr Kasparek and Deborah Padfield*
Design & layout by *Deborah Padfield*

Printed by *Kelso Graphics*, The Knowes, Kelso, TD5

All rights reserved. No part of this book may be
reproduced in any form without written permission
of the Committee of Helping Hands.

ISBN 1 900259 04 4

Eastside Community Heritage *is an established charity working across East London. Set up in 1993, it seeks to enable and encourage an interest in the documentation of local histories, cultural identities and contemporary views towards urban regeneration.*

Curlew Productions *is a Quaker publisher producing paper-based and electronic material as well as multi-media presentations.*

Contents

	Frontispiece: Old John	viii
	Preface	ix
	Introduction	1
1.	Two histories	3
	The story of West Ham	
	The story of 42	
2.	Setting the scene	23
	Steve's story	
3.	The workers	31
	Garry's story	
	Paul's story	
	Rose's story	
	Trevor's story	
	Daphne's story	
	John's story	
	Doreen's story	
4.	The inhabitants	82
	Old John's story	
	Graham's story	
5.	The neighbours	99
	Doris' story	
	Oliver's story	
	Teresa's story	
	Claire's story	
	Alan's story	
	Tom's story	
6.	The silent voices	143
7.	What's it all about?	145
	A matter of respect – Donna's story	
	Looking to the future – Julian's story	
8.	Postscript	160
	Big Alan, with thanks for the grace of God	

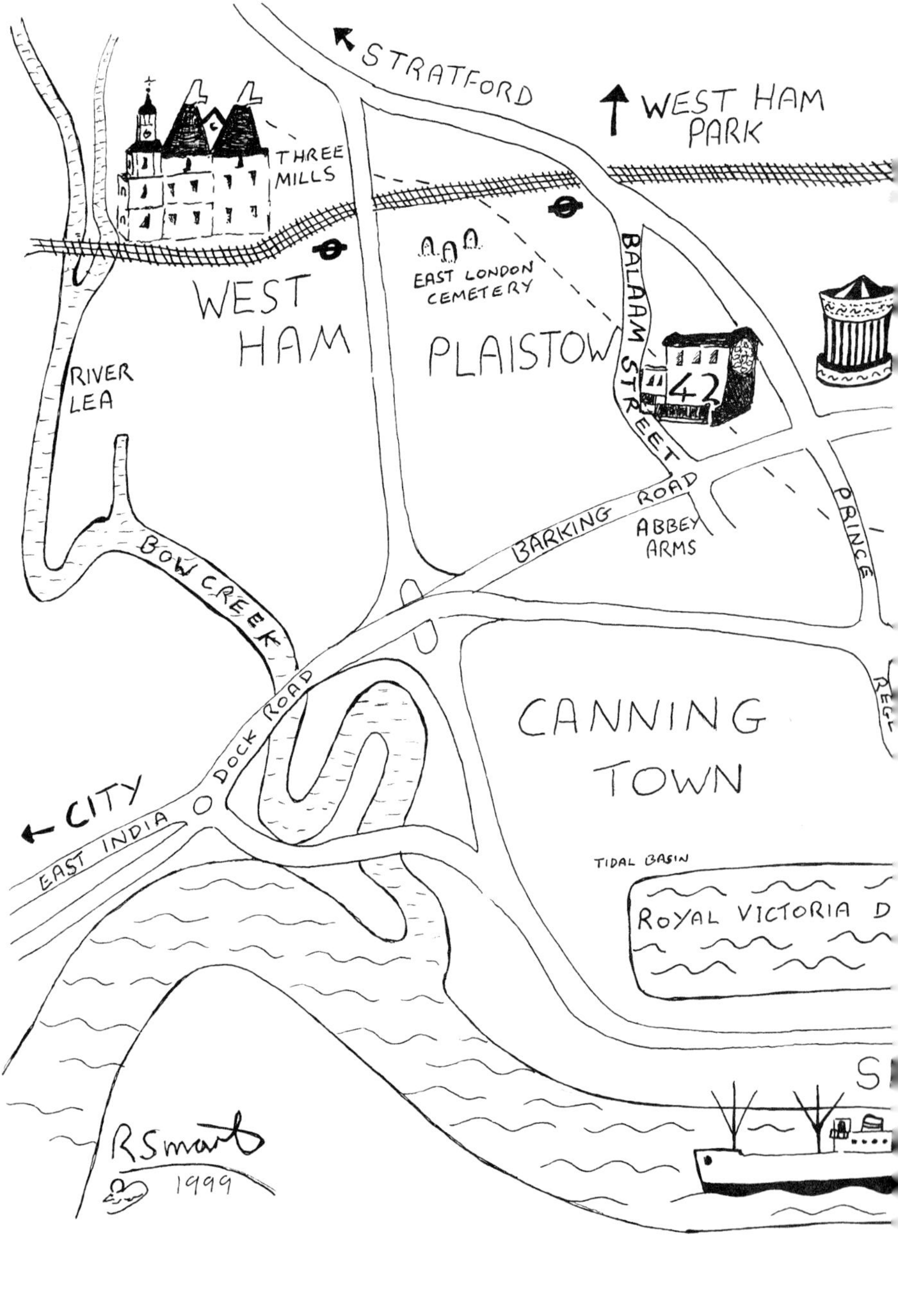

STRATFORD
WEST HAM PARK
THREE MILLS
EAST LONDON CEMETERY
WEST HAM
PLAISTOW
BALAAM STREET
42
RIVER LEA
BOW CREEK
BARKING ROAD
ABBEY ARMS
PRINCE
CANNING TOWN
DOCK ROAD
CITY
EAST INDIA
TIDAL BASIN
ROYAL VICTORIA D
RSmart
1999

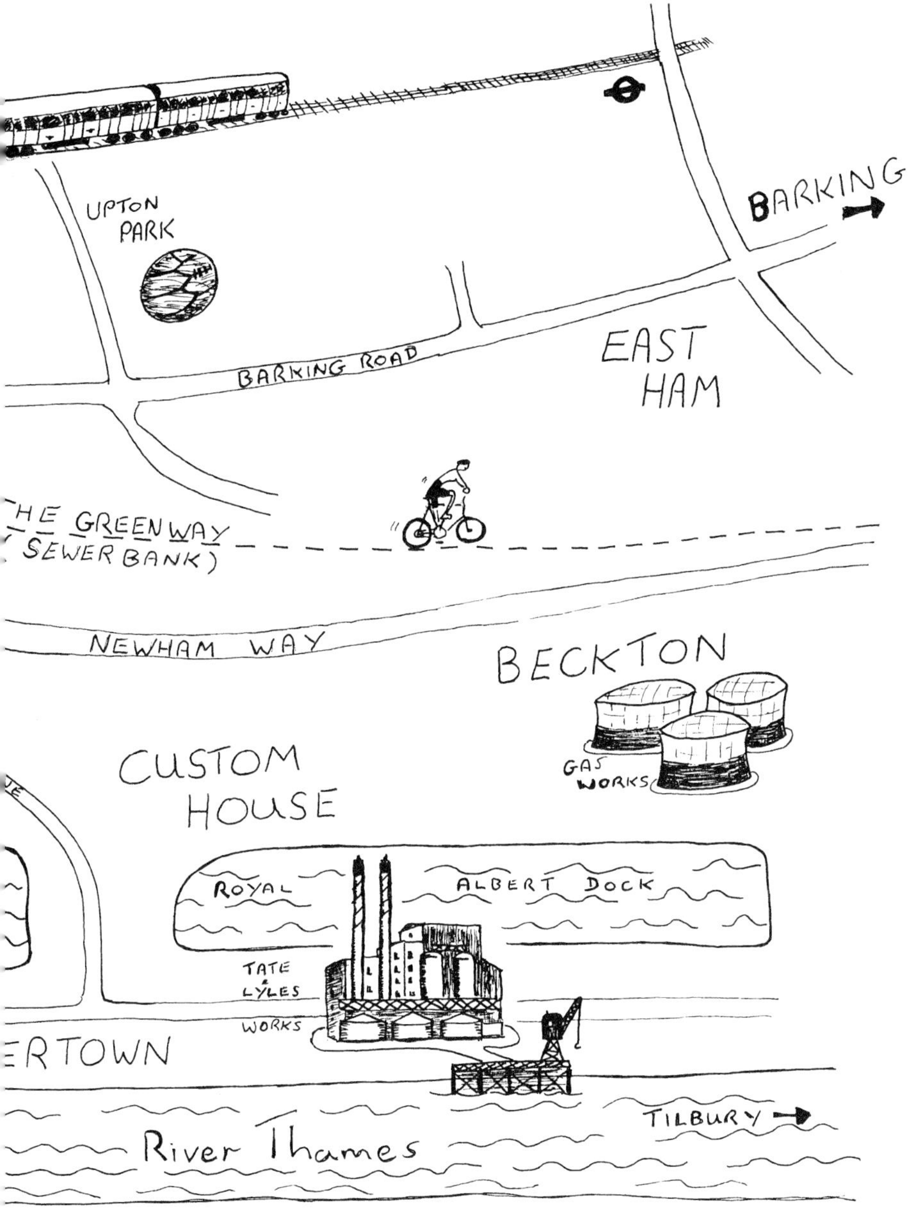

UPTON PARK
BARKING
EAST HAM
BARKING ROAD
THE GREENWAY
(SEWER BANK)
NEWHAM WAY
BECKTON
GAS WORKS
CUSTOM HOUSE
ROYAL ALBERT DOCK
TATE & LYLES WORKS
ERTOWN
TILBURY
River Thames

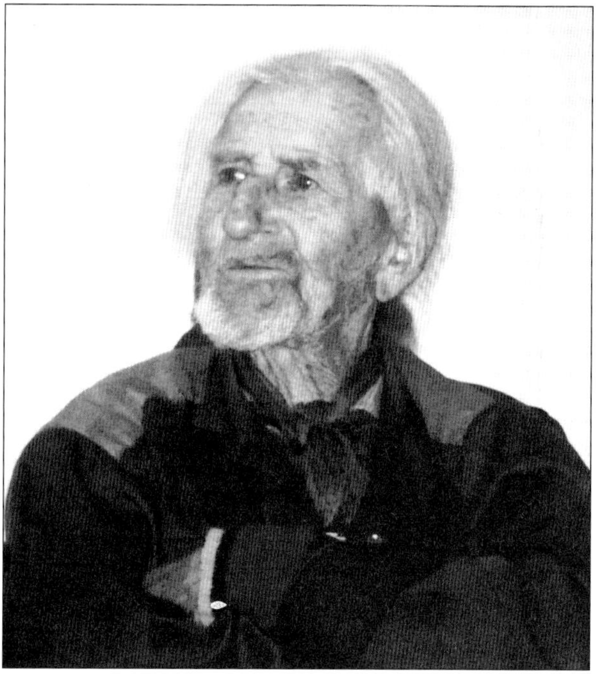

Preface

When I read these stories I asked myself, are these people ordinary or extraordinary? The more I thought about it the more convinced I was that most ordinary people live extraordinary lives. Academics may challenge me, but I can only speak from personal experience. It seems to me that those who are privileged, those who have material wealth, can (usually) buy themselves out of trouble, whilst those who can't, struggle.

I remember once listening with excitement to a young man whose car had broken down in the middle of nowhere, he was on his first real date with his first real girlfriend. "So what happened?" I said. "Well, I phoned my father, and his friend came and picked me up in his helicopter, we left the car for the poor," he replied. My ordinary neighbours would have had no chance but to struggle. They would have had to get themselves and their car to a safe place, they would have had to do so in the dark, without being arrested, and remember they won't be forgetting that this is their first date, so their story would be just beginning! So what is ordinary and extraordinary really? For some people a helicopter helping someone out is extraordinary, for me, having been a resident in Newham for over 20 years, listening to the stories of everyday people is always an extraordinary experience, an extraordinary experience I often have.

I remember going to 42 Balaam Street to rid the building of a Hammond organ it no longer had use for. Looking back, I think I probably said many things which had been said hundreds of times before by visitors, like, "Wow, I come past this place all the time... I've always wondered what happens here," and when I went into the beautiful garden, "wow, it's so peaceful, like a bit of heaven in a sea of madness." I remember looking at the people who were there as they greeted me, and thinking maybe I should stay longer, but I had to deal with the madness outside, so I took the organ and left. But every now and again when I am shopping or going about my business I hear someone shout me, I look around and I usually see a big white van going by with "Helping Hands" written on the side. There are usually a few helping hands waving back at me.

I pass Balaam Street quite often and I often think that building must house some fascinating stories. The building is a building, it is the people who bring the place to life and this book is an account of a piece of that life. It does not claim to be the definitive story of 42 or of the people of the area but it is a valuable document of the people themselves speaking, the oral tradition on the page.

I see this collection of stories as a celebration of a people and a place, a people who come from everywhere (as we all do), yet they have a single place in common. It is only through reading stories like these that you can understand what putting seats in Upton Park football ground meant to many West Ham fans who could not pay by credit card. After reading these stories, I realised how important we all are, and how important it is to record our own history. I am reminded that if we fail to record our own history, a passer-by will do it for us.

Dr Benjamin Zephaniah
East Ham

Introduction

This is the inner city, grey, litter-strewn, defined by poverty and unemployment. But within it lie stories of magic. This book is a call for recognition, a song of joy celebrating the lives which blossom here. A tribute to dignity and unsung hard work.

Behind the tall, angular figure of 42 Balaam Street, its ungainly frontage showing years of unplanned adaptation, lies a walled garden. Bigger than at first appears, it's richly planted. In parts it runs nearly-wild, tended just enough to fend off desolation; in parts it shows attentive care. Many kinds of plant grow here, some which thrive on the jostle and bustle of wildness, some which need another kind of space – the space that's found by tending and thought. A sycamore and plane tree stand strong and tall; an ornamental cherry struggles with London's worsening pollution and aridity. There's life here, made up of many lives.

Hence this book. Within these walls, there's life. The house is marked by what it's lived through in three centuries: from the comfortable days of a rural suburb through the wrenching forced birth of modern industry, to the confusions of post-modernity. There's loss of direction on every side. Now that industry has largely gone, what fuels local life? Now Newham's people derive from (nearly) every continent, what is East End identity? Where jobs are hard to find and harder still to keep, ill-paid and unalluring, where do people look for value? And now Christianity and its middle class ethic of helping the poor have lost their certainties, what is the Franciscan life, which has been here at 42 for over 100 years?

All of us who live and work at 42 came here out of need: because other things had not worked, because we were homeless, jobless, lacking direction. Each of us, in our different ways, found friendship, generous and unquestioning, unjudgemental. There's courage here, bubbling up, through the cracks in ill-fitting lives. There's glory in those hidden lives – in their honesty and strength. In love and joy, this book grows from that life, bearing witness to its indestructibility. Here, hidden in the inner city.

This book is a joint enterprise. It was Tom Nixon, Chair of Helping Hands, who suggested that we celebrate the work of the house with a millennium publication. There was not a lot of science about the selection of voices: those who were willing, who were available, who were unwise enough to run into me when I was on the prowl with my dictaphone. To any who would have liked to have told their story but with whom I didn't connect, I apologise. In a real sense, the book can never be finished: there is always more to tell.

Several people were patient enough to spend two, even three, sessions with me; with others, one was all that was appropriate. In every case, I ended with far more material than we could use. Abbreviation seemed impossible, yet it had to be done. The stories sang; as I worked on them, their rhythms and images wove themselves into my memory. My thanks to everyone for their willingness to accept the shortened versions.

The book also contains some fruits of a Tuesday writing group at the Friary: very informal, it has generated laughter and deep affection. Arnold calls us the Literary Circle. Quite right. We deserve such dignity.

Rooted as this work is in Newham, it has been deeply satisfying to join hands with Eastside Community Heritage and with our poet-neighbour Benjamin Zephaniah. Such a sense of common life and common enterprise is what it's all about. Thank you, friends.

And thanks from me to all who have let me listen. I have learned from what people have said and from the often eloquent echo of what they have not said. I have learned from what people have and have not felt able to make public, and have deeply respected their thoughtfulness. There are differences of personality at work, and differences of culture. As time has passed, my awareness of the significance of the silent voices has grown; they have needed their own chapter – their silence has needed to be heard. It is a part of the whole.

Those stories, and the conversations behind them, have become part of who I am, to my enrichment. I carry them with me as I travel on.

Deborah Padfield
aka Pebble

1 Two histories

The story of West Ham

The story of a place is made up of the story of its people. But people's lives, the possibilities and experiences open to them, are also moulded by the place where they live. That is vividly true of areas which, like West Ham, have been at the heart of that savagely abrupt incident in our history, the industrial era of the nineteenth-twentieth centuries.

Indeed, the development of West Ham as a Victorian industrial suburb was essentially a piece of crude profiteering by those in a position to benefit from cheap land, demand for cheap labour and the desperation of the under-employed. The result was a locality so heavily dominated by heavy industry and an unskilled population that it lacked the variety of employment and skills which alone could give it protection from the jagged transformation of Britain from industrial to post-industrial economy. Ecological and economic systems both need diversity to survive crisis – diversity of a kind which allows the disparate parts to work together, not destroy each other. Modern Newham is hugely diverse; only time can tell if that diversity will be creative or destructive.

West Ham's high day came and went with staggering speed. In the 1830s, it was still a rural parish. Today, it is a ward in the London Borough of Newham. The opening of the Victoria Dock in 1855 and the docks' closure in the 1970s-80s effectively bracket its heavy industrial history, both growth and decline carrying heavy human and ecological costs. Yet out of industrial decline have grown new patterns of community, new ways of coping and living.

Unlike the northern cities, West Ham has no proud place in England's industrial folklore. And as for Plaistow, right in its centre, not even the recorded station announcer on the District Line can pronounce it right. It's Plarstow, not Playstow. Yet a council pamphlet of 1910 was not absurdly entitled *West Ham, the Factory Centre of the South of England*: save for Bristol it was the largest county borough south of Birmingham. The docks built in this marshy intersection of the rivers Thames and Lea were major employers from the 1850s, supporting and being supported by a host of heavy – and heavily polluting

– industries, notably chemicals, engineering and metalwork, food, drink and tobacco; textile and leather trades; printing.

But West Ham is far older than the docks. Even football has a long and chequered history: it first appears in the records in 1582, when a man was murdered during a match. More illustriously, Empress Maud in 1100-1118 built the first bridges across Bow Creek and Channelsea. She gave the Abbey Mill and land in West Ham to Barking Abbey in return for maintaining the bridge.

Plaistow is first mentioned in 1414, the name deriving either from the shape of the settlement around the central green – the "plaice of play" – or from the family de Plais. Balaam Street appears earlier, in 1364-5, maybe named after the Balun family who had lived here since at least 1183. In the 1740s, Plaistow was the largest settlement in the parish, made up of the triangle formed by High Street – in the 1500s called Cordwainer Street after its leather workers – North Street and Richmond Street. Letters were collected daily in Plaistow, Upton and Green Street by 1692 – twice daily in Stratford and West Ham villages. Balaam Street was an offshoot to the south-west of Plaistow. By their pubs shall ye know them: by 1742 there were 14 pubs in Plaistow, including the Black Lion and Coach and Horses on the High Street, the Greyhound on Balaam Street and the Crown (later Abbey Arms) at the end of Balaam Street on what became Barking Road. In 1776, the Greengate Inn – first known as The Gate – appears in the records, to the south on the edge of the marshes.

The marshes... Dickens came here for the wild, bleak climax of *Great Expectations*: Plaistow stands right on the southernmost point of solid Essex soil. By the sixteenth century, much of the marshland running down to the Thames had been reclaimed for arable and meadow, though reclamation continued right into the nineteenth century. London was just to the west, market for all goods. So in 1853, the parish of West Ham still had 1,100 acres of arable and market gardens, 2,600 acres of meadow and pasture, eight acres of woodland – the southern boundary of Epping Forest had been the present line of Romford Road – 62 acres of domestic gardens and orchards, and 82 of osiers and reeds. By 1905, there were just 127 acres of arable and 51 of permanent grass, mainly to the west of Prince Regent Lane. Land was now valued for other purposes.

Rural Plaistow was prosperous in a way that industrial Plaistow was not to be. Between the 1500s and early 1800s, West Ham was home or holiday home to wealthy London

Allotments east of Prince Regent Lane

merchants and professionals. From mid-eighteenth to mid-ninteenth centuries, Plaistow was the largest and richest village in the parish. But the world changed around it: by 1818-19, Stratford's rateable value was nearly twice that of Plaistow.

With the Thames marshes to the south and no direct road to London in the west, Plaistow was cut off in a way that Stratford, with its bridge over the Lea, was not. Only in 1810 was an iron bridge built over Bow Creek, linking Barking across the marshes with the Commercial Road. Public services have had a short life in Britain: like most roads, New (later Barking) Road was built for profit, by the Commercial Road Turnpike Trust, with a tollgate close to the bridge. Not until 1871 was the bridge taken over by the local Board. Beckton Road east of Prince Regent Lane was a private toll road until 1931.

Barking Road was important above all for the future Canning Town and Silvertown. Plaistow remained to around 1840 a prosperous suburb, home to some well-known names. Constitutional theorist Edmund Burke lived here from 1759 to '61, as did chemical manufacturer Luke Howard from 1772 to 1864 and musicologist and publisher John Curwen from 1816 to 1880. Sir Henry Tate of sugar-refining fame brought wealth to Silvertown, his home from 1819 to '89; Keir Hardie and Jack Jones were members of Parliament for the constituency.

With the '40s came a change of gear. The beginning of that decade saw the completion of the railway to Stratford, built by the Eastern Counties Railway. In 1843, life stirred further south as a branch line opened from Stratford to North Woolwich with a station on the Barking Road. The North

Woolwich Land Company promptly bought and developed land between the Barking Road and the Thames. Much earlier, small mills on the branches of the Lea had had their little wharfs. Now, in 1848, C. J. Mare & Co.'s shipyard was opened on Bow Creek. Work was begun on the Royal Victoria Dock, and in 1852 Mr Silver brought his name and rubberworks to the area. The career of West Ham's south-west periphery as cheap home to noxious industries had begun. In 1857, Dickens wrote in *Household Words* of this "place of refuge for offensive trade establishments turned out of town – those of oil-boilers, gut spinners, varnish-makers, printers, ink-makers and the like... No wonder that the stench of the marsh in Hallsville and Canning Town of nights is horrible."

Swiftly now, workers' houses spread. By 1855, streets snaked north and south-west of Plaistow. In 1858, the village joined the steam age with the loop line to Barking through Plaistow Road station. The scene was set. Between 1870 and 1901 West Ham was transformed, all available building land being taken by rows of small terraced houses. In 1841, the population was 12,738; it grew steadily to the year 1871, then faster in the next three decades. In 1911, the population was 289,030.

But Plaistow itself has never been home to heavy industry. Inevitably, that was concentrated in a crescent down the Lea from Stratford – with its road and railway to London – to Canning Town and Silvertown, then along the Thames to Beckton. Plaistow had its works, to be sure, with silk weaving through the 1500s and 1600s and again from 1882 to 1943, Luke Howard's pharmaceutical factory from 1797 to 1805 and a small railway works in Plaistow Road from 1875 to 1934. Above all, it was the centre of a sizeable West Ham printing tradition. When the Society of the Divine Compassion set up their Whitwell Press in Balaam Street in 1901, they were following two other nineteenth century Balaam Street printers, W. H. Thodey and Son and W. S. Caines Limited. There were others, too, not least the musical specialists Curwen Press, in North Street, Plaistow.

On the whole, though, Plaistow became a tightly packed dormitory for West Ham's west and south. Industry brought wealth to some, but bare subsistence to most of those who flocked here in search of work, casual in the docks and largely seasonal in the gas works and brick yards. The locality struggled with heavy poor rates to support its un- and underemployed people, amongst the poorest of whom were the Irish Catholics clustered mainly in the south-west. Father Andrew of the Society of the Divine Compassion wrote in his diary of 1894 that "I have found families without even the light of a candle sitting silently and starving in the dark."

The authorities, reluctant to risk driving away industry by regulation, turned a blind eye to pollution and bad working conditions. Challenged in 1895 about manufacturers' failure to observe the Smoke Nuisance Act, a councillor responded, "where would West Ham be but for the factories?" The Council merely tried to contain the pollutants, pushing heavy industry into the west and south.

In the first flush of growth, building was unplanned and uncontrolled; not until 1856 was a local board set up under the 1848 Public Health Act, its work bedevilled by lack of resources, local politicking and corruption. Silvertown sprang up in the 1850s without any provision for sewage, while new factories and docks along the Thames blocked existing sewage outlets. The great Northern Outfall Sewer of 1855 (now "the Greenway") was the first real response to the problem, but its aim was mainly to ease the sewage nightmare of all north-eastern London. West Ham grew without adequate water supplies; without baths; without adequate firefighting services; with sickness. In the epidemics of 1848-54 over a third of all deaths were caused by disease; in the 1890s in the poorest areas around the south-western periphery of the borough, over a fifth of children died before they were two. A smallpox hospital was opened in Western Road, Plaistow in 1871, followed by a second just across the road in 1877. But an area of tight-packed housing was not a clever site for such a hospital, which by the turn of century had become a single Plaistow fever unit.

Southern West Ham's housebuilding boom was a tale of the quick buck and of spreading slums: land was cheap, industry wanted plentiful, low-wage labour; hence uncontrolled profiteering. There were building firms aplenty, but few lasted long. Profiteers with few skills employed poor materials to throw up rows of terraced houses – plain, flat-fronted houses of 4-6 rooms from the 1840s, embellished with ground floor bay windows between 1875 and 1890 and with two-storey bays from 1890. From 1900, the bays became square. Designed as family units, these ignored the fact of poverty: multi-occupancy became the norm. Only with the coming of council housing from 1901 were self-sufficient flats built, each with its own outside bathhouse. In contrast, in West Ham and Upton to the north, wealthy families bequeathed land in the 1870s to provide parks, a magnet for more well-heeled owner-occupiers.

In 1886, the parish of West Ham became a municipal borough, recognising just how revolutionary was its rate of change. The next ten years laid the foundations for a dramatic development of public baths, hospitals, electricity supplies, trams and sewage. This is the point at which local government changes gear, from the piecemeal inefficiencies and personalised politicking of a parish facing problems far beyond its means, to the party-politics of a London borough. Through the 1890s, organised labour was taking shape. Keir Hardie is the big name, but more significant was the growing power of the unions led by Will Thorne – who worked at Beckon Gas Works – of the Gasworkers and Ben Tillett of the Dockers. 1894 saw the formation of the United Socialist and Labour Council, made up of the moderate Independent Labour Party, the more radical Social Democratic Federation and the West Ham Trades Council. In 1898, West Ham experienced the first Labour majority of British local government.

West Ham was awash with unemployed people desperate for work on any terms. And so the Labour Group looked to strong unions and to year-round work which would reduce dependence on casual labour. Hence, in 1898, a wholly unionised Works Department was set up to undertake all Corporation projects; it was to observe a 48-hour week, pay a 20 shilling weekly minimum wage and provide two weeks' holiday. Labour and other Progressives demanded that gas, trams and water be municipalised. The notions of public ownership and services were, albeit slowly, being born.

The Labour Group came to power through an alliance of radicals and moderates who believed better conditions to be in everybody's interests. But the struggles within the group were profound – and long-lasting. Did the Labour Group aim to improve conditions under capitalism or to overturn capitalism itself? Was it the party of organised labour, in which case what were its relations with un-unionised workers, often the poorest of them all? And if no private companies were willing to do essential public works at union rates, was it more important to have the work done or to hold

> **A first time**
>
> A Sunday morning in September, cold. We had heard we had a flat in Beversyde Point. Walking up the unfinished staircase, I entered the almost-finished flat.
>
> Light, light and more light. Windows everywhere. Views looking over to Kent to Bostall Woods up to the Post Office Tower. It was a wonderland, a dream – could this really be our home after Whitwell Road, the four-roomed terraced house, narrow garden and front view to house opposite?
>
> So much space, unbelievable views – here up off the ground it was like being in the clouds.
>
> Strange. I haven't thought of this in years. The wonder of my lovely flat which I have grown to accept and take for granted.
>
> Through 30 years there have been many moments of love and joy, but nothing quite like the childlike excitement of that first visit.
>
> *Brenda*

out for union pay and conditions? Such disputes found practical shape in 1898-99. Then, in 1899, the establishment hit back, founding the Municipal Alliance against Socialists.

The conflicts within and surrounding turn-of-century Labour were also cultural. In 1899, an Alliance councillor pounced on the fact that the journal *Freethinker* was openly available at a borough library, rather than being accessible by request only. The churches were in an uproar; the national *Times* ran the story; in 1899 *Freethinker* went back to its coy resting-place under the counter. But the controversy expressed a deeper division. Church-people were significant players in Labour's victory; what were they to make of socialists who poked fun at the YMCA – the "Young Men's Chloroforming Association"? In 1900, Labour lost control of the borough council; not until 1919 did it regain control, never (to date) to lose it again.

West Ham's slums were an intractable problem whoever held a majority. After the spate of late-century activity – the first council houses were built between 1899 and 1905 – little was done to alleviate the housing situation until the 1920s. It was much the same story with transport. Between the 1880s and the early twentieth century, services had gradually improved, with horse trams running from Canning Town to Greengate in 1886; all tramways, now in borough hands, were extended and electrified in 1903. The District Line was extended to East Ham three years later, the year in which motor buses made their appearance. But public transport was not to change significantly again until the coming of the trolley-buses in 1937.

So too with street markets. West Ham's first market had made its appearance – on Tuesdays – in 1253 by royal grant. It lasted longer than a more light-hearted enterprise, a Whit Monday pleasure fair set up in 1806 opposite the Greengate Inn. But such pleasure was disorderly, immoral; North Street Congregational Church took a lead in fighting the fair and it was duly suppressed in 1809. Other, more utilitarian, street markets sprang up in the latter part of the century, always attracting controversy as lovers of order confronted the traders. When in 1886 West Ham became a borough, the council tried (illegally) to evict the weekly traders; the police refused, and a policy of containment held an uneasy peace until some shaky regulations came into force in 1891. By 1911, Rathbone Market was alive and well in Canning Town. No more action was taken until the 1920s, when the council received statutory powers to regulate street traders.

After the highdays of the late 1890s, local politics became a minority interest, bedevilled by very low levels of voter registration: turn-out at the 1939 municipal election was the smallest out of nine great English towns studied that year. Only the trades unions and the cooperative movement seem to have had widespread local support.

Yet West Ham was no dozy place. The people who had flocked to Greengate pleasure fair also enjoyed their sport. West Ham United Football Club became professional in 1900, growing out of three amateur teams, the St Luke's, the Old Castle Swifts and the Thames Ironworks. It joined the League in 1919. In 1894, West Ham had the oldest swimming club in Essex; Plaistow continued the tradition, providing five members for the 1936 Olympics water polo team. Plaistow's E. H. Temme was the first to swim the Channel both ways. Nor was it a godless borough, every conceivable Christian denomination having its place of worship here.

When West Ham's soldiers returned to their "land fit for heroes" after the Great War, though, it was to a land of slums. Overcrowding and unemployment were more bitter than ever. So at last, from the late 1920s to 1939, West Ham undertook major slum clearance and road building – including in 1934 Silvertown Way on its viaduct and bridge, unblocking bottlenecks caused by narrow swing bridges and crossings over docks and railway. In London, only Bermondsey had a larger slum clearance programme. Schools were founded, adding to those already provided by the borough or its churches.

Other faiths were to come with post-war immigration. Yet West Ham was already no stranger to racial diversity. In the 1700s, potato growers and calico weavers had imported Irish labour, causing conflict in years of high unemployment. In the late nineteenth century came other migrants, particularly Scottish workers for jute-spinning and sugar refining. German scientists were employed by the chemical industries.

These "foreigners", though, were not the only outsiders. Of those who lived in West Ham in 1900, the great majority were themselves newcomers. Such large-scale, high density industrial development was a new phenomenon. Even those whose families had lived in West Ham parish were newcomers to West Ham the industrial borough. East End culture in today's Newham is hardly more than a century old, a product of diverse people and cultures thrown together by their common need for work.

Yet the trauma of change was hardly beginning. The second world war and its aftermath altered the face of West Ham past all recognition – both its buildings and its people.

Over a quarter of all West Ham's housing was destroyed by bombs. The heaviest industry and worst slums fared worst, Tidal Basin losing 85 per cent of its houses and Beckton Road 49 per cent. The 20 years following 1945 were a time of intensive redevelopment. Over 9,500 council dwellings were built, 8,000 of them permanent. For many local people, the memories of those 'temporary' but often long-lasting Nissen huts is still green. The Keir Hardie estate was to become one of the largest areas of public redevelopment in the country; at first providing houses with gardens, it became increasingly high-density as the 1950s wore on. The 1960s brought the 200-foot tower block, the most notorious of which, Ronan Point in Canning Town, collapsed after a gas explosion in 1968. Later public housing reverted to low-rise patterns.

Firms had still been coming to West Ham through the 1920s and '30s despite the slump, and most of its industry survived the war. New firms carried on coming, and surviving. Up to the late 1960s, engineering and metalwork were still the most numerous and successful newcomers, followed by chemical works. Construction firms, too, were big employers, as were the docks, the railways and road haulage companies, right through to the '60s. From the mid-'60s, though, the picture began to change again.

So we come to the final stage in the story so far. In 40 years, West Ham has again been transformed beyond recognition, physically, economically and culturally. In 1955, the docks – the largest area of enclosed water in the world – and industry were at their peak. The big firms provided a stable basis; most had local roots going back 25-50 years even though some names had changed as they became part of multi-nationals: Tate & Lyle, Standard Telephones & Cables, Unilever, Harland & Wolff.

Then came recession and restructuring. Between 1971 and 1982, manufacturing jobs fell by 42 percent in the borough. The docks which in 1950 had given work to some 50,000 people employed about 2,000 in 1981. In the ten years from 1965, about half the working population of Canning Town experienced redundancy as industry contracted and the docks began to close. From the early '90s, medium and large industries fought to survive recession, replacing workers with technology. To the west, Hackney and Tower Hamlets have their share of City commuters as well as developing their own financial and service sectors, not least in Tower Hamlets' new Docklands; far less so

Beversyde Point and single-bayed terraces beside the Greenway

in Newham. Here, there was little by way of an adaptable skills base to attract new capital. By far the majority of jobs lay in small business of less than 20 employees, largely low-paid and low-skilled. And so in 1993, Newham had the sixth highest unemployment rate of all districts in the country.

Old skills were becoming redundant, old working relationships dying with the rapid reduction of union power – once so central to West Ham – in the 1980s-90s. Pay was low: in 1991, a third of all Newham households were receiving income support. Whereas nationwide the number of working women was rising, in Newham it was falling.

Partly, this links with the other great change for West Ham: the growth of "ethnic minority" communities, with their own attitudes to the roles of women. In the 1950s, workers particularly from the Caribbean brought welcome labour to docks and industry. Like London as a whole, Newham's population was falling between the 1950s and '80s, as better-off white workers migrated to the leafier suburbs; in Newham, they were almost entirely replaced by immigrant communities. By 1996, Newham had the highest proportion of ethnic minority peoples in London – just over 50 per cent, mainly in the central and northern areas, including West Ham. It is a complex of communities, above all from the Indian subcontinent, the Caribbean and East and West Africa. Commonwealth citizens were followed in the 1980s and '90s by refugee groups, especially Tamils, Somalis and more recently Turkish Kurds and peoples of the former USSR. In Plaistow, neither Asian nor Black communities predominate:

New Vic School, Prince Regent Lane

a complex mixture live alongside each other.

The result is a population both richly diverse and hugely vulnerable. Linguistic and cultural differences, added to lack of high-tech skills and the racism of employers, make job prospects thin for the people of West Ham. In the 1990s, dramatically fewer asylum-seekers have received full refugee status. Far more have been granted exceptional leave to remain, giving them no right of reunion with their families and no certainty about how long they will allowed to stay. Insecurity is a hallmark of life.

And Newham is an extraordinarily young borough. Potentially, that is a strength if young people can find active places for themselves in the world; otherwise, they remain desperately vulnerable. The white population is ageing – more than one in five white inhabitants have reached retirement. But over half the non-white residents are under 30, less than four in a hundred of them being over retirement age. Since the late 1980s, Newham has had the second highest birthrate in the country. In an area where few houses have four or more bedrooms, one result is multi-occupancy, particularly in the Asian communities.

Young, strong ethnic minority communities which are growing and set to grow more: religion may be dying elsewhere, but in Newham active membership of religious groups has expanded through the '80s and '90s, particularly amongst those groups which tend to be poorest, the African, Pakistani and Bangladeshi communities. If individualism is a hallmark of much white religion, in Newham faith – including African and Afro-Caribbean Christianity – tends to be strongly communal.

Within this, families matter. Although fewer young couples have been marrying in the last 15 years, Newham has fewer births outside marriage than the average – and more young divorcees. Young black and Asian people are trying to reconcile the conflicting cultures in which they live, the traditional demand for childrearing within marriage being continually in tension with modern strains on marriage. Out of the clashes within and between communities, new social patterns struggle into life.

A century ago, a generation was growing up in West Ham who, unlike their parents, had been born into a densely-packed heavy-industrial world. Likewise today, a generation is maturing which was born into the multi-ethnic, post-industrial hot-house of West Ham. A century ago, the Council had set up its first municipal Works Department, the trades union movement was young and strong and the idea of public services was gaining confidence. Now, a New Labour council is privatising those services in quest of "Best Value" – value for money and flexibility. Social and political activity is shifting back from the public to the private sector – to the plethora of religious and community organisations alive in multi-ethnic Newham, and to the alliances they form.

The future lies partly outside local people's control – as with the Jubilee Line extension to Canning Town and Stratford, which is opening those areas to white-collared commuters and pushing up property prices. In part, the future is with the young people of Newham and the confidence with which they tackle the coming century. And, in part, it is with the always-hidden life of that core of under-skilled, under-employed people, coloured, black and white, whom the economy needs yet never values. In the end, it is on their ability to keep on living, loving, laughing, in spite of the system, that the peace of the city depends.

The story of 42

In February 1876, Plaistow witnessed the arrival of strange figures: its first English monks since the Reformation. They came to Ivy House in Balaam Street, four or five Brothers and a few "externs", members of the Guild of St Alban. The GSA Brothers had a dual aim: to become part of the locality and to draw the locality into their life of prayer and fraternity. In their first two years, they enrolled some 50 men and lads as "Associates", able to share in their corporate worship and to come to tea, that Victorian high-point. In 1879, a hall was built in the garden for entertainments and as a clubhouse for neighbouring men and boys. But it wasn't all tea and cakes: around the 1880 general election, they became increasingly politically active. Theirs was an experimental life, maybe testing out the limits of the acceptable in late Victorian Plaistow. In 1882, the lease of Ivy House was surrended and the Guild of St Alban departed.

But Anglo-Catholicism was still sparking new life. In 1894, the first novices of the Society of the Divine Compassion took their vows at Pusey House, Oxford. Brothers and Sisters, Franciscan in inspiration and black of habit, they founded a mixed house in Meredith Street, Plaistow in that same year. The SDC described itself in 1908 as seeking "to live a poor life, sharing the privations and discomforts of ordinary poor people" – "a neighbourly life". So they came to the parish of St Philip and St James in Plaistow, known as "Essex over the Border", an area of serious unemployment, poverty and ill-health. The SDC brothers saw the devastation wrought by unemployment – "the ruin," they commented, "that comes through not being wanted."

The Brothers trod carefully. Much of the spirit of the Guild infused the SDC – but not its party political involvement. There were open debates for men and a Ragged School, tea in the refectory and visits to the workhouse; there was the establishment of the Whitwell Press and, later, of a watch-repair business employing three apprentices in Balaam Street. Work-creation was an economic and theological good. "The need of this age," the SDC believed, "is to emphasise the dignity of labour – not to beg with the beggar, but to work with the worker... Love for the... oppressed and starving... is best expressed in helping them into work, and, by example, influencing them to do the work conscientiously, as for God." A Protestant work ethic, studded with colour and music by Anglo-Catholic ritual – and with the pageantry of street theatre.

The SDC took to the streets with tableaux intended to relate the bible stories to everyday life. Ever-optimistic, the Brothers saw these as "a kind of parable of what their own lives should be. Men who labour on the roads and in the docks, women who work in their homes, girls who go daily to the factory

Brothers to...

If you go right back to the beginning of the Brotherhood of St Francis in 1921, they formed a constitution in just two paragraphs. One was to do with the Brothers, and the second paragraph concerned the Wayfarers. So the Society was originally made up of Brothers and Wayfarers. Right back to our very roots, we saw that the Brothers were insufficient if we were on our own; we needed that other group. It is important to me that I am not Mr Damian – I'm Brother Damian, brother to... Not simply in title, but in reality, to all.

Now we are becoming more creative in community, and less institutionalised – that's what the western world is really interested in. Here at Plaistow some people are residents, some are more needful people, some are Brothers – so, in a very quiet way, something special has emerged here which is not based in constitution, but in the needs of the people themselves. I'm not sure you can say "this is what we want". Rather, this is a gift which has emerged and has been worked at slowly. I would want to honour that gift.

One of St Francis' often-repeated sayings is, "Preach often, sometimes using words." It's not what we verbalise that's going to count as Franciscan. It's in the making strong of other people, and the encouragement towards dignity and drawing people out, which I believe was Jesus' own method. He was never putting people down, but rather drawing people out. It's out of our love – and more particularly God's love – for other people that we hope to see them grow stronger. We should enjoy that. And there must be some way, if the relationship is to be a real one, in which we can receive as well as give. That's absolutely fundamental. Sometimes it is quite uncomfortable to be on the receiving end; and sometimes it is just nice! Equality – in the end that is where we all stand before God.

That is where we've got to get to. The real challenge is in recognising our equality under one heavenly Father. Goodness knows how we can work it out! But it's of the very essence of faith.

Brother Damian, SSF

and the shop, children who trudge off to school – these make manifest the Christian life... [A]s we have seen God made manifest in Christ so we should see Christ made manifest in Christian lives." And so the Brothers combined prayer and printing press, and confronted the real insecurities of life in the smallpox wards of Plaistow hospital. An SDC publication of 1908 commented that "it is a curious and instructive experience to find a monk in his habit working at an electric printing press." Instructive also for the monk, one hopes.

In the 1890s, the SDC inhabited three houses on Balaam Street. Then, in 1908, William Gordon Norman of 42 Balaam Street, auctioneer, went bankrupt. The house – probably built in 1760-70 – and garden were bought for £1,100, the money being raised by an appeal in the *Church Times*. It became the House of the Divine Compassion. As a matter of principle, the Brothers refused to instal a bathroom until 1953, this being a luxury enjoyed by few local people.

Father Andrew SDC died in 1946, leaving just two Brothers behind him. They approached the Society of St Francis, founded in 1929 and now the strongest Anglican representative of the Franciscan tradition. Father Joseph SSF and two novices were sent to Balaam Street, other Brothers soon following. In 1958 Father Barnabas, last of the SDC family, died.

And so the House of the Divine Compassion entered its next chapter – with renewed vigour but much continuity. The Brothers SSF kept the Daily Office in their chapel, singing mass and evensong in nearby St Philip's. Links with the local hospital were retained, Sunday worship being celebrated in Howard Road maternity hospital. St Philip's had set up Guides and Brownies in SDC's time; in 1954 SSF added Scouts. And under the dynamic Brother Geoffrey, known for the unexpectedness of his ideas, plays on a cart took the bible message to the street once more. St Philip's needed rebuilding, and the foundation stone was laid a year after the coming of the SSF. Youth activities, sport, drama, a "fellowship" for young wives: much vibrancy. In the '60s, a time of struggle as evangelism bore meagre fruit. Protective wire was put on St Philip's windows. But in 1963, a pageant was born and a newspaper launched – *Roundabout*. These were the days of maximum visibility, the "Brown Brothers" out on the streets and in people's homes. Brother Nicholas with his finger-puppets, Brother Howard who worked in a factory: these names recur in local memories. In 1965, 42 was reorganised to create more accommodation for Brothers, the chalet being built in the garden. Another room was later added to house the chapel, moved now from the main building.

With Brother Leo (rt) in front of the mural in the garden

Brothers – no Sisters yet. SSF had a tradition of sharing its life between Brothers and lay guests, the "Wayfarers" – but women could not enter the House beyond the entrance parlour. In 1953, though, a Franciscan play was performed in the garden to which women were invited; Brother Matthew later recorded that "some ladies were heard to express joy at seeing, for the first time, the chapel 'where Father Andrew prayed'". But in 1983 Sisters, members of the Community of St Francis, came to live at 42.

In the late 1980s, the House began to build up a stronger partnership with local people. In 1990, Helping Hands was founded, its aim being "to promote any charitable purpose for the benefit of the residents of The London Borough of Newham especially the Plaistow area, and in particular the protection of health, the advancement of education, the relief of the elderly in need, and the relief of poverty, sickness and distress." It was an organisation run by unemployed local people, using their skills and commitment to answer the needs of vulnerable neighbours. In its value statement, Helping Hands said simply that

"we believe in the value of every human being and the importance of giving each individual the opportunity to grow. In partnership with others, we seek to provide high quality services which are accessible to all within the community."

Increasingly, the House was now home to two kinds of community, the Brothers and Sisters, and the local people who gathered here, worked here, found home and family, work and value, with each other. Increasingly too, the real sense of purpose lay with this lay community. In any live society, priorities shift over time; there are areas of growth and of decline. So with the Society of Francis. Plaistow was no longer at the heart of its work. In 1995, therefore, the SSF decided to close 42 as a Friary.

Yet it did not close as a Franciscan house: the life of Helping Hands, held steady by the dedicated presence of Brother Julian, was too vibrant for that. For an uncertain year, Helping Hands continued its work, the House becoming home to an increased number of people who found themselves, for a variety of reasons, in need of a place in which to rest and re-focus. After that year of uncertainty, a covenant was drawn up under which Helping Hands and this shifting household of sojourners could continue as joint users of the House, each paying a rent to SSF.

A different kind of Franciscan life was gently growing, tentatively sending out buds. Some have borne fruit; others have not. The House is experimenting with a life shared by people of different backgrounds, cultures, classes – individuals discovering, using and valuing their skills, giving freely and receiving freely. 42 has a quality of timelessness: there is no goal to be reached, but just life to be lived, setting its own rhythm. The garden is part of the House, and the garden teaches such timelessness.

This is an experiment in not being in control: none of those who live at 42 own the House or have a *right* to be there. That is difficult, because the need and the right to possess a home and job are deeply entrenched in our culture. Yet it is also freeing. Nothing is permanent – neither the presence of individual people nor the pattern of life within the walls. People come, people move on, and the pattern shifts. A different kind of security is operating.

And so we live and work here, sharing the House and garden, the bottomless sack of tea bags and the indefatigable kettle. The life of the House is the life of its people; hence this book. But the life of the people is shaped, in part at least, by the House which we have encountered – hence also this book. A celebration of its life.

Long'uns

Looking back over the years I recall a shopping expedition which, for me, was an outstanding landmark, a gateway to the future, an assurance of fruit to be tested, a promise of riches to be won, an earnest of life beyond, of challenges to be accepted, of battles to be fought, of causes to be vindicated. Well, that's how I saw it in those far-off days of childhood innocence.

In days very long gone by, boys left school at 14 years, sometimes even earlier, and it was the custom for boys to wear shorts until leaving school. That meant that knees were exposed to public gaze, and knees, like the back of your neck, attracted dirt. However well-intentioned you might be, this always seemed to happen – to me, anyway. And so on going home the first comment invariably was, "Just look at your knees." In vain I protested innocence of knowing how they attracted dirt; in some mysterious way they did.

Now, on the way to school I had to cross the Bricklayers Arms coaling station where Southern Railway engines dropped by for their MOT. This was an opportunity never to be missed. With my mates, I clambered on to the bridge with notebook and pencil noting names and numbers of 2-6-2s and other engines. Unfortunately, we had to contend with the school bell which always rang when we were most engrossed.

Clambering on bridges was seen as dangerous and was therefore forbidden by school, but we reasoned that while appreciating the love and anxious care of the adult world we could take care of ourselves; and the five-minute sprint on hearing the school bell was the finest training for school athletics. Anyway, it was outside school hours.

The foregoing may seem longwinded but the scene had to be set for the great event. Schooldays were days of innocence. The only worry was getting your homework done in time, or perhaps the serial at the local flicks which had left the heroine bound to the railway track, and us curious as to the locomotive that was thundering towards her.

Well, the inevitable happened. My mate called for me, and I stared. He was in long'uns. The age of innocence was in retreat. We both stood on the threshold of manhood. He was leaving school but I was doing a five-year course. For how long would I be expected to wear shorts?

My fears were put to rest when my mother decided a trip to the tailor's was on the agenda. The tailor's shop was a large private house in Peckham. Most of my aunts dealt with him. The business was a sort of Provident club where contributions were paid in during the year. The smell of new cloth was beautiful. What is more, I was to be allowed to choose my own pattern.

The tailor called for the assistant who stepped forward with his tape measure around his shoulders. He took measurements. The first steps to emancipation from childhood were about to be taken: inside leg measurement; arm measurement; back measurement; a fob pocket or eyelet in the waistcoat for my watch chain; and button hole in the lapel of the jacket.

The parcel arrived. I tried it on.

The trousers had turn-ups; no belt of course. Belts went with grey flannels and blazers worn at the seaside. No zips, not yet in fashion, and not altogether respectable with trousers.

The waistcoat had an eyelet for my watch-chain, now suspended across my chest. I had dispensed with the fob pocket in the trousers.

So there I stood. No longer would my knees pick up dirt; anyway they would be hidden. But no longer would I go scrambling up bridges taking locomotive numbers. A new era had opened up. From now on long'uns were in and I would be caught up in a man's world. You could hardly escort a girl in shorts; at least, not in those days.

Brother Arnold SSF

2 Setting the scene

Steve's story

Steven is a curate in East Ham, a mile to the east of Plaistow, but he was born on Balaam Street in 1970. With his open face and laughing voice, when he visits the Friary he's immediately at home with whomever he finds there. And as an insider-outsider to the area, he looks at it with a shrewdly observant eye.

I was born in this street, in Howards Road hospital. My mother's family have lived in Canning Town and Plaistow for 100 years. Two years ago I had a great great-aunt living in Balaam Street, and my great-aunt still lives round the corner, in Hayday Road.

So Plaistow is very much part of my history. We lived near to the sewer bank till I was three. My parents had a shop around the corner, a newsagents. So that was my first years, wander down the street to the greengrocer, talk to everyone in the street. Then we moved to Canvey Island. Practically everyone you meet on Canvey Island moved out from Plaistow! My mum had always gone to Canvey Island for day trips, my great-grandparents took their honeymoon on Canvey Island. It's really the poorest of people of my parents' generation who are still here. When you look round this area, you find a very elderly white generation, most younger people have moved here from elsewhere.

I used to come and spend every school holiday with my great-aunts. It was fabulous, every day they would take me out somewhere, I've been to all the major museums, art galleries and so forth in central London. But we also went a lot around this area, East Ham, Upton Park. The Woolwich Ferry was always a good day out.

My dad has since had other children, but until I was 18 I was an only child. My great aunts spoiled me rotten, I had a fabulous time! My great-aunt lives in a street where in most houses the families've been there for about 50 years, quite a few are Irish Catholics. So I know everyone in that little block, I speak to all the neighbours, go in the corner shop and so forth. Until very recently, there were no black people in that street. My great-aunt's part is still a sort of all-white street, with the exception that one woman up the street has a black grandchild. This child who is very much part of this traditional community is the only black kid there.

My parents always did factory work, and later my mum worked in old people's homes and now runs a day centre for the elderly. And my dad, he trained as a welder, a youth worker, computer programmer, and then a psychiatric nurse, at 40 he did a degree, and now he's working in a peanut factory! My mum's dad worked in the docks. My dad's dad has always been a wheeler and dealer! He is very skilful with people, he's quite persuasive, and my father also. I've sometimes thought that the work I do probably involves using a lot of the skills that they use, though we've done very different things.

My parents were young when I was born, we've always been able to discuss things. They were divorced when I was about 14, but they're quite friendly with each other. We did a lot of things together. My great-aunts also, they were a big influence on me. A lot of what I learnt about generosity came from them, and politenesses, as well as East End superstitions like not crossing anyone on the stairs and so forth. But they would often talk about political things, particularly in the Thatcher period!

And church was very important. I went to a Church of England primary school, I met the vicar through that and I started to go to church. Occasionally my parents would go, but not really. So I kept going there basically until I was 21. I didn't enjoy my secondary school. There was no discussion in relation to international issues or politics or religious matters. The church was very involved in politics and community life. I had a lot of opportunities to put ideas forward and do things – even though I was 12, the vicar said let's set up a youth group, and encouraged me to help.

After I left school I went to Durham for a year, didn't particularly like it. There was a lot of heavy racism and xenophobia, sexism and homophobia in the college I was in. It was really horrible.It was 80 per cent private school and that was quite difficult for me, being with people whose experience was quite different, who held views which I found very difficult. So I decided not go back.

The timing wasn't right, I didn't feel able to face all the things that I'd been struggling against.

So I went back to Canvey and worked in a drop-in for young homeless people. I did a lot of political work, in relation to CND, homelessness, the Gulf war, the environment. Heady period, really. I learnt a lot of skills in terms of being involved with groups, which I'm finding very useful now.

In that period I decided to go forward for ordination. I'd always known the Brown Brothers, but I didn't meet any of them until it was recommended at that time that I should get a spiritual director. So I wrote to the Friary and said, because of the Plaistow connection I'd be interested in someone from here.

I didn't want to go to college straightaway, I wanted to get a bit more experience. Basically I'd lived at home, I lived with a girl friend, then I had a flat on the Island, so I'd never experienced community life, and that's something I quite fancied. I thought it would be nice to discover a bit more about where I've come from.

So later I said to Julian, "I fancy spending a year in a community", so he said "well all sorts of things would be possible, you could go to the Solomon Islands." And I said "well you know, I was thinking about here." And he said "oh by all means, come and see what you think, see what we think." There were were two Sisters in those days, and about nine Brothers, it was always great fun. So I came a few months later to spend a year.

I did a few things in the house and locally with HIV+ people, and a bit of hospital chaplaincy. It was interesting, because I didn't have much personal space. There were tensions, and that was a challenge! I suppose I sort of wondered about the religous life, whether that might be something for me, and I wanted to experience it as a means of discounting it. Which in the end I was able to do. Thankfully!

And afterwards I went to a village in Essex, Nazeing, as a parish assistant. I spent a year there, and then I went on to Lincoln Theological College, and when it closed I went to Cambridge. But in vacations, I came and stayed with my great-aunts in here Canning Town.

At Upton Park

Community is important to me. Canvey Island has quite a strong sense of community, and then I experienced community quite differently here, and also in Nazeing. And then I suppose again at college. And now – married with a child! One of the things I enjoy about the East End is the sense of identity, community. There's a lot I love about the East End – certain things it's easy to criticise, but there's a lot I enjoy about the indigenous white culture, the humour, the honesty, the generosity.

The Friary, over the years, although it's changed a lot internally, it's always been a sort of stable place, somewhere to drop in. It's important for me. It was lovely to leave from here, the day I was married, especially as I was born in the street. And it was great living here, because I've met people from all over the world as well as a huge variety of people locally. There's the indigenous white culture, and I also love the fact that Newham is very much a multi-cultural area.

Sometimes I hear resentment. A number of white people have moved out, so their old friends are not around. But that's cos they've moved! That's why the area's changed, because they've moved! To me the multi-cultural is a positive thing, it makes the area vibrant.

In a way, a lot of what a lot of what white people think they miss is more present now than it's been for a while. Because people do spend a bit of time out the front, standing outside or sitting outside the house and that's something I remember a lot. When I was a child, elderly people sitting outside their houses, chat to people as they pass by. And I've seen elderly Asian folk do that, round where I live in East Ham. And the emphasis on family and things like that are very evident with black and Asian families.

I'm interested to think about how East London came to be a sort of homogeneous community. It was really only about 150 years ago that people moved here, and when they came, they were strangers to each other. And that community developed quite quickly. I think it is possible, in 30 years time or so there'll be a much stronger sense of a unified culture. And a lot of it's to do with shared experience, especially in schools.

I noticed when I was coming back in vacations that Canning Town and Plaistow have changed. From having basically no black people, they've become very African. Down near Hermit Road, you'll have three Kenyan people sharing one room, someone working a night shift, someone's working days, someone sleeps on the floor, there'll be three-four upstairs, you'll have a Nigerian family in another room, so you'll have about ten people housed there, which probably hasn't happened there since my grandparents were young! They were a family of six, they'd be upstairs, and there'd be another family of maybe six downstairs. That's how a lot of these houses were occupied in the '30s, it's getting to be a little like that.

And people's attitudes change quite quickly through mixing with people. My great aunt, she will always talk to children, regardless of their colour. There's a lot of that. You hear racist talk, but it doesn't match up to how people respond when you're talking to them on the buses.

And of course, the effect on church life has been extraordinary. Newham's reckoned to be the most religious borough in the country. And a lot of that is Christian. But I think in a way, now, the big religious difference is between liberals and those people who liberals like to call fundamentalists. I think there's a lot of Muslims round here who have much more in common with a lot of Christians than is sometimes realised, in terms of their understanding of the world or sense of faith, or sense of the importance of family life, importance of education and the lack of respect for Western democratic notions – freedom of individuals and so forth.

In St Bart's Centre we have another four churches meet. There's a Jamiacan Pentecostal church, there's a mixed one, there's a Nigerian church, and a Coptic Orthodox church, and in other church centres in East Ham we've got a Kenyan church, a Ghanaian one. In this area, I think there's much more confidence about being part of a faith community. It's quite contrary to notions of secular society. People can be quite bold about their religion. That's respected by people of different religious traditions, I think, much more than those attempts to work at finding common ground. I don't think those attempts have been very productive.

It's a lot to do with people who've moved in, who tend to take worship much more seriously. But the indigenous white population is generally speaking not church-going, though it's important to get the kids baptised and so forth. The future will be multicultural, needs to be. I suspect there's a better chance of that attracting local people.

A lot of the religion in this area is very much integrated with national identity – ethnic identity – family life and so forth. That's a good thing. They're using their own language, I think that's good, because people like to worship in their own language. It is a problem if people don't feel welcome to worship elsewhere. But offering buildings to those churches is a good way of existing churches telling them they're welcome.

In white indigenous communities, there are a lot of traditions, even though they're new ones. You find a lot of symbols that connect very strongly with people. But you wonder what those symbols mean. A popular symbol is a teddy bear. It's everywhere. If you get a frame for a child's baptism certificate, no cross on it but teddy bears. And cross-stitch is very popular, little teddy bear designs. What does it signify? With the Christian tradition, you can say this is light, or water, it works out in this kind of way. But this teddy bear – I find it odd. It has some kind of significance, but people don't really know why. Even if people have a sense of what it means for them, there's nothing to inform them about why it's important. And that's what's so strange, to have a tradition with no sort of guidance.

A lot of it doesn't mean anything. I mean fair enough, but it doesn't really help us think about how we live our relationships, how we engage with politics. How we understand how our communities are changing. I think a very positive thing about religion is that it gives people guidance in how to live and that guidance, I think, is very lacking in a lot of traditional culture. On the other hand, people have quite a strong sense of what is important.

I think it helps this area, having West Ham. I think it's very significant. At the end of the day, it doesn't help you to transform the unjust structures of society, but I'm very enthusiastic about football. It does engage people with chance and highs and lows, because a lot of contemporary culture is very predictable and controlled. Everything's the same. You go into one Burger King, it's the same as every other. So I wonder sometimes whether people are more affected by predictability than they realise, and if the growth of football culture isn't in a way a response.

I think it is growing, football, not just white, across the board. Last week, West Ham did a thing, "Asians in Football", to try and promote Asians in football, though it's a struggle for them, I think. And we play in the park every Sunday, and it's so nice to see people there, really a mixture of people playing.

It's important to me, work-wise, to be engaged in this sort of context, because I have an understanding of what I promote about it and criticise about it. It's given me experience of engaging with issues which are increasingly important, like multiculturalism. And I love it here!

The Friary – to me it is a very interesting symbol of changes. You find here, in one building, what is dispersed around the community, all sorts of people relating to each other. It's quite significant – to find refugees, mentally ill people, people who have been round the area for years, you find people who have moved in, you find a class difference here, age difference and so forth.

And I think that's quite special, to be able to experience it in one place – with all the humour! There are probably few places where people are able to just come along and experience that kind of variety. With nothing particularly to do or to get out of the situation, I think that's quite important.

So, long live 42!

Finding a way

The mortgage was due, the water rate bill hiding behind the clock. He who held the purse strings was despondent. We had got to find a way.

A six month old baby in a just-paid-for pram. Things looked bleak. The menu for the day: fish paste sandwiches, and an apple. The only one happy: the baby.

Family conference. My mother, a widow, was working herself, could not help with the baby. In the local paper, a small toy factory in Stratford advertising for home-workers painting toys. We could paint. Off we went and came back with two boxes, supposed to be 50 soldiers to paint. When the boxes were opened one contained toy Indians with instructions. Faces needing seven colours. The other box – mean-sized bottles and a small brush.

It took hours. Back to the toy factory. Thoughts of beef stew, carrots and dumplings. Perhaps we could pay the water rate.

The fat gentleman looked them over. Quite well done, said he, but this is only a test piece. We do not pay the first consignment. I tipped the lot on the floor and walked out with dignity. Carrot soup and dumplings.

Back to the papers. Only addressing envelopes, not much money there.

Next day, a neighbour said her niece had just opened a shop but there was no one to look after her six month old baby. Thought I – I was a twin and my mother managed. When you are mixing a bottle you may as well do two. Two lots of nappies... I had been brought up to think nice thoughts. Forget nappies till we come to them.

I took the job. The boys were company for one another, and Graham went home at 7 o'clock in the evening. Water rates paid.

Soon after, Arthur, who was training as an engineer in Stratford, heard that a barber was needed at the hospital. He had previously been a barber. Twice a week after training he cut patients' hair.

This went on for three years. Bills paid. We had found a way.

Susie

3 The workers

Garry's story

Garry's dark, not tall, stocky. He walks decisively, head down, like a small battering ram, and speaks readily, his voice very expressive, acting out his mood. As he speaks, the memories and emotions seem to live – as does the humour. He's a bit of an actor – acting himself.

I was born on the 29th October 1962. The seventh child, with five sisters and a brother. Me earliest memories is like me first Infants' school, then there was the circle of people, like neighbours, friends. I had me sister, she was a year older than me, she was in the Infants, that was like a comrade. There was a big whale, we used to jump on the whale, if anyone went on that side the whale they was in the water, they drowned. There used to be an iron fence separating the Infants and Juniors, and I remember standing at the fence, watching the older boys play football, and I couldn't wait to be a Junior so I could play football.

Great memories. It was a big house, big garden, we had an apple tree in the garden. Being the youngest one I was still at home with me mum when my sister was started Infants. We had – it was like magazine rack only it was more sturdier, and she used to put mats and rugs over it, beat them to get the dust out, and I had a string and I tied it on, I'd sit on it and pretend it was an horse, and I'd get hold of the string and like jog along as if I was riding an horse. We always had fish on a Friday, cold fish, with parsley sauce, and obviously Sunday dinner. We weren't religious as such, my mum believed in God but that was as far as it went.

And then I had to start the Juniors, I remember crying the first day, terrifying, really was. But you made little friends. It was a rough school, bullied quite a lot, not me personally but they mixed, like, from seven up to 11, so there was boys with knives. You never said nothing. It was an old Victorian school, it was about five storeys high, and it was old lead pipes, with sinks.

That's where I made me initial friends, guys that I was hanging around with up to me 20s. And then they closed the school down, and we moved to Colgrave School, and then we went to New Colgrave. Started getting a bit mischievious when I was about nine, I got put down a year, so that affected me education as such. So anyway, after leaving there, I went to Rokeby, Stratford, I went with a whole crowd of mates. I done very well in the first year. And then like 15, 16 of us used to hang about all the time together, and like the six weeks holidays, for tuppence, we used to get on a 69 bus and go to Chingford Mount, and then pay two pence to go to Woolwich Ferry. Used to go out egging – well, was really just getting up the trees, all thorny. And we used to go over to River Lea, used to kill water rats. First real taste of nature, being like in the city.

I wasn't allowed out on a Sunday, cos it was like bath day. Up till I was 14, had a tin bath in front of the fire. There was no hot water, it was all boiled up over the stove. My mum just kept doing it, you know, get up, get breakfast, get the kids off, start washing, preparing, do the tea. Just day in day out thing, seven kids, that's all she really knew, everything was involved round her brothers and sisters and her children, it was all family. And we had me Nan and Grandad round the corner, me uncle and aunt over the road. Me dad died when I was 15, he was 55.

And then the third year I just totally went wayward. I started hanging about with kids that was in the fifth year, and I started breaking into shops, staying out all night, then doorstepping, nicking bread, you know, eggs, bacon – they used to leave all that stuff on the doorsteps. It was just, oh, sod society, I'm having fun. And then I started getting arrested. So when I was 14, I went to stay with me sister up in Yorkshire. And that was real country, that was sheep, that was curlews, kestrels, rabbits, rabbit burrows. Camping out like with me mate, it was beautiful, clear skies, just used to lay there looking up at the sky, talking about UFOs. He'd lived on a farm all his life, and he showed me round the country. See a deer, live – I don't know how to describe it. It was like a big deep valley, and fern trees everywhere, and there was this deer, just come out the woods, looking round.

The only thing, I had to start school up there, which was one of the worst experiences of my life. There was this stuff that I'd never learned, and I got put in with all the kids that don't want to learn. And I started hanging around with the kids on the estate and that. So then I started getting nicked for criminal damage, theft – just petty things. So it was decided that I should come home.

And then I got arrested. I was 15 in October, me dad died on the 18th of December, and I went to court about the 22nd, and I got put away for three months detention centre. I was crapping meself. That was a dreadful experience. I didn't really get bullied. I wasn't stroppy, but I didn't cow down, if you see what I mean. One kid threatened to do me one night and I laid awake – cos anyone they wanted to give a clump, they used to clump them at night. So that was an horrible night. The worst experience I had, somebody done something and they punished the whole dorm, so that rather than they punish you, they know that night you're gonna get a punch. They made us pull back the mattress off the beds and you know like the wire squares, had to stand barefoot on that and hold your boots out for about five minutes. And to me that's just sort of torture, it's just wicked. I'll never forget that. There was no education whatsoever, no English, nothing. Cleaning duties, I had.

Your supper was a bread roll and cup of tea. Wasn't allowed sugar or nothing. That's why I don't take sugar in tea. And if I have bread and butter, cup of tea, I still get that sensation of being there. And left-over dinners was all mashed up, baked into like a little cake, and it was called a brick. So your breakfast was like porridge, brick and cup of tea. And they used to say like three and a brick and it's going very quick, that means three more breakfasses and I'm going home – a brick and I'm going home, and that was it. Cocky little kid. Got on the Waterloo train, and it's all bowler hats and *Times*, spitting on the floors, you know, like – all you middle class bastards, yeah, I've just got out of nick – they must be used to it at that station, little villain, seven o'clock in the morning. Never got in trouble since. I wasn't going back there. I got a real sense of what freedom is. I remember laying on me bed, just wanting to play football with me mates, I was only 15.

And then it was like last year of school, I remember the teacher said,

"Garry, if you just sit at the back, don't disturb the class, I'll let you do whatever you want." Cos I was cocky little... And my mates, they was all working, they was going to discos – all I wanted to do was earn money and go out with me mates. So I went straight into work when I left school, repairing tarpaulins with palm and needle, like a sailor. That was it. I was a man then. Started paying rent indoors. Going out Friday night, Saturday night, Sunday lunch time drink, have your dinner, football, kip, normal thing. And that was it. It was like me life. And I remember when we left school, everyone had work, except one kid that was unemployed, and that was such a strangeness. I mean why don't you go and earn money? Cos there was tons of work, factories everywhere.

I was very shy at that time. But I had girl friends. The first, about 16, the first girl I really went out with. Till then, I was just like knocking about with groups and that, having little snogs. This girl I went out with for a little while. Nice girl, as it goes. Ohoh, I'm getting in love again!

And then I got a job as a porter in Queen Mary's Hospital. It was quite an experience – taking bodies to the morgue, picking up a plastic bag, and it's got half a leg in it. Then I watched a couple of autopsies. That was gruesome. The first time, there was a woman that had stomach cancer, when they cut her open, it was the most dreadful smell. That wasn't a bad job. I started drinking heavily then, thinking back now. I was mixing with men been drinking for years. The nights were pretty quiet. So I used go over the pub, and the bleep would go off, so you'd put your pint down, walk over the road, go and get the bottle, take it over to the ward, go back to the pub. Drink started getting bad then, looking back.

Then after that I done painting, for about a year. Total novice. I was working with a load of Irish guys, drinking, drinking, £25 a day, I was 19, 20, still living at home. And I met a girl that had a little baby girl, 18 months, lovely little girl. I think – always wanted a little kid. And I settled down a bit. And I would say drink destroyed that relationship. Wasn't that I was violent, just loud-mouthed – didn't knock her about or anything. Come home from work one day, and mum went "oh Sharon's left," and I went "oh well, if she's gone she's gone." I regretted that, at a later date. Yeah.

I was on a big job at Maidstone, painting, then I worked with the guy that was the foreman, just him and me. And he'd been doing it for years, he was up me arse all the time and I

Channelsea, looking towards Canary Wharf

hated it, so I quit that. Then I got a job as a sales rep, loft insulation. It was a good scheme as such, but all you was worried about was just getting people to sign. And there was old girls could hardly see, couldn't really follow what you were saying, and the bloke would say get them to sign. So I didn't feel comfortable, plus I wasn't earning, so I went into the other side, I went into insulating.

I done that for a while, it was interesting, going up in people's lofts. And – can't really think of a job now till I become a panel-beater, sprayer, it was my sister's boy friend, his firm. And I didn't know nothing about cars, nuts and bolts, didn't know which way they go in. It really did click – car's damaged, you repair it, and it goes out looking brand new. Got a buzz. Really did.

So then I met Angie. We wanted a child – she got pregnant and then life was different. I asked for a wage rise, and it was like – whoo! – manhood now, responsibilities. Soon as Catrina was born – best six weeks of me life. Angie had a bad time, so about half hour after Catrina was born, Angie rushed to the theatre, I was pacing round with just Catrina, she opened her eyes, looked at me, and I was like, "might be just me and you, kid." Anyway, she come through it. Life was sweet, I had a job, I had a real woman, baby, it was really good. Life had changed totally.

And then me guvnor – once the baby was born, he's like "I've got you over a barrel now." He really used to tear into me. So I give in me notice. He thought, no way is he going to leave, but I did. Just too stubborn. It was quite good, you can cope if you're sensible. It was a lot of time with the baby, and

Angie. And then the garage changed hands, and I went up there, and I ended up being there a year and half. But me and Angie split up. It was a mutual agreement, which I won't go into, because it's personal, it's a two-sided coin, that one. But – it was quite a blow. And then me drinking really took off. Not because like Angie or anything, but, here I am now, I'm a free man, aren't I? And I was earning bundles of money.

Then me Uncle John kept saying to me, about this place, the Friary. He said, you just pop in for a cup of tea. Oh, boozers' low-life, I ain't going there, sitting around having cups of tea. And then I wasn't working and I was getting in a rut. So I come down and have a little chat with Julian, and he said what skills you got, and that was it. He sent me on a couple of decorating jobs, and then slowly I got involved. It was an outlet for wasted energy – and then I got involved more with the people. And then I regretted it and then I loved it then I regretted it then I loved it! And I love the people here. When I come here, I was very aloof. It's like, oh, riffraff, losers. Yeah, I know, "I'm special, I can do things, I don't need to sit round here" – and that's what I do now, sit round all day like an idiot! I've achieved my goal in life, to be a drop-in!

And then when I broke me leg, Julian said if you wanna, stay for a while. But breaking me foot – it slowed me down, emotionally and mentally as well as physically. And I wanted better of meself. But then obviously took the cast off and took me conscience off and I went back to me wayward ways! But it did have an effect on me. It was a break from duty, really. I could leave it to one side, focus on me for a while, till courage to go and sort what I had to sort.

Used to go round me mum's every Saturday, me sisters, me brother, nephews and nieces, their kids. Go and pick Catrina up, West Ham Park for half hour, then around to me mum's. But drink and drink and drink, got worse and worse, till – foolishly told Catrina's grandmother, I said "look, me drinking's got out of hand, I go to AA..." Then I went to pick her up, there was a notice saying she weren't well, then a letter come from the solicitor saying you can't see her no more.

The key word for me, it's self-destruction. I've got that button inside me that I press. If it's gonna hurt me, I'll do it. Always bin like that. I can't work it out. It's not like me dad was in and out the nick all his life so I can say "oh it's his fault". No way. It's me. But at this present moment I'm looking forward to staying off the beer, exercising, playing the guitar, writing. I'm in a good stage, and I want it to last. All I'm looking forward to is eating properly, sleeping properly, being more creative. That's it. Being creative.

I never read a book until I was 22. And then I read Joe Orton, *Complete Plays*. I loved the stuff. Because it's all dialogue – I just want to absorb the characters. And then words, words come into me life! And now, I love words, the way you can articulate yourself. It's what it's all about. I was about 22 before it really kicked in. Dictionary was me first bible. When I was about 20 to 23, I got a dictionary and I wanted to study all the words, know what they meant. Since then I've read Dostoyevsky, *Crime and Punishment*. It was very relevant at the time, because at the time I bin seeing a marrried woman for a year. And the actual punishment is the guilt that goes on in your head, oh, all the paranoia. Punishment, I know what punishment is, it's guilt and paranoia!

What do I hope to be? Me! At one point I was into technical drawing. Straight lines and parallels, all that. It's just correct, and everything was in line. It's like religion, everything lines up, that's the way I see it. Geometry was very important to me as a child. Everything made sense, everything lined up. And science, loved science. really did. Like life, got to make some sort of sense of life. That's the point. It's not what your parents tell you. You've got to make sense of life.

And I regretted like, when I got a bit older, I thought oh, education! I wish I made the most of it. Knowledge was my first god. I just wanted to learn. All of a sudden, like out of the blue, oh, hungry with a passion. And when I say with a passion, that means more than hunger, that's not eating for like three years. Prior to that, I was just like a fun-doer, you know, live for the moment, have a laugh and blablabla. But then you had to make some sort of sense of what's going on. It just clicked. I've not stopped since. P'raps it was coming to meself. I discovered meself. And that was it – I don't want to stop learning, I want to be wrong for ever. Do you understand that? I want to have somebody say, well you're wrong there, and I go, oh, that's a good point. And I can develop it. I never want that to stop. Just seeing beauty. Discovering beauty like language.

Guitar? Oh, I was 19, just learning from books, sit there and learn the chords. Studied a bit of the rudiments, playing melodies and bass lines. Now, I know I can create a song, if I come up with some lyrics and put a melody to it I can put chords to it. Oh, music is something that I'll never express. It's just been like the biggest opening. I pick that guitar up now, and I'm going places, it's unimaginable. That's the truest sense that I've found God in. And that's the real beauty of my life, that I can tune into that, I've got the knowledge, I've studied. Took like six solid years of graft. But now I'm benefiting, cos I can pick the guitar up, all I've got to do is strum one chord, then a few ideas come into me head, then I just follow the patterns, ad libbing.

Never bin ambitious. I'm into people, into relationships. I'd rather be there for someone, you know, in whatever sense. Another form of creativity? Yeah, I imagine so. To give myself, be receptive. As long as I enjoy it – it may sound a bit selfish, but it's the truth. As long as I satisfy me own soul, that's all I'm here for. I feel very predetermined. This is Garry. This is what I've got to be, it's not a right or wrong or anything. I ain't steering the ship. I'm going somewhere and I'm gonna learn what I've got to learn along the way. That's it. I believe in that.

When I got to the age of 22, round about, I decided, I said "I'm knocking all the walls down, everything I've been taught." And it was like – start afresh, show me the evidence, give me an argument and I'll weigh it up. Was just like I'm starting from me, and then I can be me, you understand? I think that was me first rebirth. I started to question things rather than just argue for no point's sake. Wanted to know – and try to understand. Get the shapes back together.

And that's exactly what I'm going through now. Shapes are changing again. Here I am again. All goes pear-shaped. Like again I've gotta make sense of what's happening. The building blocks keep changing. I'm not moaning, thank god that's the way life is. I'd rather it be this than what it was stagnant.

The crux of it all really, when it comes to me last building blocks it'll be same as the first ones, and then I'll die. I've been fucking about with it for years, keep changing them about, but it's the same structure. The Master Plan. I believe that. Total order out of chaos. They keep changing the rules, but the answer's the same. Something like that, anyway. I ain't worked it out for myself yet. I'll build a song round that!

Paul's story

Paul is small and wiry, in his 50s but ageless – indestructible. Very hoarse voice, a croaky laugh; tough-guy act; in awe of nobody. He lives on tea – sugar bowl empties itself into his mug. He speaks in jerks, pure East End. "Eh?" he says, hand to hearing aid. "Eh?"

'I was born in Howards Road hospital – yeh, Howards Road, you know where the ambulance station is, just by there. And lived in Forest Gate all me life. Up to the time I got married, in 1961. Yeh, me and me sister, me mum and dad, they're dead now. Me sister's still alive.

'Dad? Worked in the docks. Yeh. He did. So did I, till it all had to go down to Tilbury. And couldn't get down there, cos me old man had a motor, like, and I couldn't drive, so I had to knock it all on the head.' Laughs. Croak-croak-croak.

When he started work, he was – '15, 16, something like that. You know, like, I've given up welding now, cos me old man dying, you know. Ship repairs, that's what I was in. First off, like. And that's why I give it up, cos dad died, you know, and then mum died, what – week, fortnight after him. And I was right up the stick. Oh, see, 1978, something like that. Yeh, I used to work wiv him, see. And as I say I had to turn it all in after he died, so I haven't – you know. That's how it went.' He stops dead. Pause.

Has he been back to work? 'No, no. Not welding, you know. I could do, I suppose, if I put me mind to it, I suppose I could get another job, but... Not at the moment, I can't. No, well I mean it brings back mem'ries, you know what I mean. And I get upset, don't know where I am.

'Me grandmother and me grandfather used to take me down to Clacton, well, me grandmother used to take me, every year, for a holiday like, you know, and I enjoyed that when I was young. Me and me sister, took us both, yeh. Oh, very good she was, I liked that.'

But 'even she went, see. She went down to Finchley, to see one of her cousins, one of my aunts, used to work in a linen shop, clothes shop I mean, and she died while she was in Finchley. Was the last I saw of her.

'Upset about that, well, not so much as Mum and Dad dying you know. But I mean, they all seemed to go at the same time, and it knocked all the bleeding go out of me, my life, it has. And I still ain't really got it together yet, you know what I mean. Losing all your fam'ly, like, bar me sister. She lives in Ilford.

'Mischievious little bleeder, I was, get up to anything you like. You know, running in and out other people's houses, things like that. Breaking a few winders. Playing cricket in the street, and football. You know.

'Used to bash me up something else! My sister, that was. Cor. "I'm coming to get you," I'd say. "Nnnng!" "I'm gonna have you today," I'd say to her. Fat chance. Crunch! "Bully!" And then she'll holler out, "Mummy, he's hitting me! Mum, he's hitting me," she'd say. And I'd never lay a finger on her. She always used to take me sister's side, me mother. And the old man, cor, Jesus. "What've I done, Mum?" Then me sister'd say "you hit me!" "No I haven't," "yes you have," "no..." Give her a clump when me mother's not looking. "He's done it again, Mum," she'd say. "Why don't you leave her alone," me mother used to say, "Well, she started it!" "Why don't you leave her alone?" That's how it goes.

'School? I went to Harold Road. I went to Elmhurst Road, first. Then I moved from Elmhurst Road, you know where that is? Harold Road, that's where I left school. Forest Gate, it's only just round the corner to where I was living. Well, you know, not too bad, I s'pose. Fights in the playground, and gawd knows what else. Fucking balls through the winder. Ball, where you got a post with a square thing on the top, and you gotta hit that with a ball, and there's a geezer in front of that with a bat, that's gotta hit it. Wonder what they call that. Running all round the playground.

'The headmaster's name at my school was Thurston. Yeh, Thurston. And he was a git. Always used to pick on me, always. "Pick on somebody else." Get the old stick out, hit you round the old arsehole with it. Oh, gor. Put your hand out, whack! I said, "I'll have you one of these days." And I did. Yeh, I did, oh yeh. Bash, smack. "Now you won't do that no more, will you?" "Yes," he said, "I will." Who won? I did. First round, but he did the second, and all the rest of them. Yeh. That was just before I left school. "Oh, I'll have you before I leave this school." Cornered him in the playground, didn't I. And I've gorn thump! "You shouldn't do that, you shouldn't do that, you ain't gonna do that to me, are you?" Scared of him? No, nobody was. He thought he was one, but he wasn't. Oh, was all right, I s'pose, me school days. But...'

His mother? 'Ah, she was great, her, she was, smashing. Handle me all right, yeah. She did, n'all. I never took a lot of notice of me dad, you know what I mean, I was Mum all the time. Oh yeh, I was Mummy's boy all the time when I was young. Yeh. Good, it was. I don't like talking about it a lot, you know what I mean, cos it starts me orf.'

He went straight into the docks? 'Not straight away, I didn't, no, I used to work in the baker's. Then I had the chance to work with me dad in the docks, and I was there, what, oh, nearly seven years I think, and it all started going down to Tilbury. Now if I want a job back in the docks, I got to go down to Tilbury. But there's no way of getting down there. So I've had to knock it all on the head. I didn't want to, but that's the way it turned out. You know what I mean. I've turned it up now, give up wiv it now. I wouldn't go back there, because bring back too many mem'ries.

'Yeh, I got married, yeh. That turned out well and all. Doing all right. That's the only bit, me mother, me parents died, both of them almost at once, as I say, Dad went first, and then me mother went. Fifty-two, Dad was, when he died. And then me mother, she died about a fortnight after him. Unexpected, yeh, yeh. That made it worse, you know what I mean.

'Today I'm on me own, like, you know. Wiv my boys, like, look after me well now. Five boys, two gels. That made a – ding-dong, eh? Five boys and two gels. Oh, my eldest boy is 30-odd I think. Can't remember the youngest. He's – I don't know. I'll have to ask him! I don't think he knows, either, tell you truth. My eldest boy's come to live with me now. And I'm glad really, you know what I mean, cos I can look after him and he looks after me. And that's how it goes.'

So Paul's been out of work – 'About, what, 12 years. Twelve years last month. And that's why, cos the old man died. I could still do what I used to do, you know what I mean, like, but I don't fancy it at the moment, cos I'm not prop'ly over it.

Paul in the drop-in

I wish I was. But as it happens I'm not. You only come back to work when you feel – but that's what I'll do eventually, I think. Go back.

'Really upset me when me mum and dad went. Me grandfather, me grandmother, died, me mother, she's died, me old man. All go. Phew. So I got it all on top, you know what I mean. And it's getting to me. They say, "why don't you forget about it?" my boys, "why don't you forget?" I say, "how the fucking hell" – pardon me – "how can I forget?" I don't wanna forget. Cos it's fam'ly, see, my boys – all aunts and uncles aren't they?

'Can't sleep. I can't. Can't sleep. I dose meself up with tablets, to make me sleep, you know what I mean? Tablets to make you sleep, tablets to wake you up, that's how it's got me. Mem'ries you can't forget, can you? Keep them on all the time. Grandmother and grandfather, happy mem'ries, me mother happy mem'ries, me old man as well. You know what I mean. There were never arguments, anything like that.

'And – it's a case of whether I wanna go back or not. In a bleeding stew now, aren't I? If I go back into the job I was with the old man, that'd upset me more than it does now. If it gets better, all well and good, I'll go back, but if it doesn't, you know.' Good mates, him and his dad? 'Oh yeh, yeh. Bin working for the old man all his life, well, best part of his life, and we got on well, no arguments – well, not always no arguments, you know what I mean. Less arguments than I had with me mother. And me sister. And I really don't know whether to go to work or not, back to work.'

How did he come to the Friary? 'My boy introduced me to Julian. Yeh. I dunno how he found out about it. My eldest boy, yeh. And that's the way it's turned out. When I got a job here, Rosie was on the desk, you know Rosie, she was on the desk then, well I bin here ever since. About five years. I'd go back to work, but I'm not ready yet, know what I mean. And maybe I'll get over it, maybe I won't. And that's me, see.

'I'm glad I come here. It's helped me a lot, you know what I mean? Coming to terms with me mother and father, and me grandmother and grandfather, come to terms with it, you know. And I'll be ready – well, not ready, you can't never forget it, can you?... Think of the bright side of it, or the good side. Best way, innit? And honestly I don't know what I would've done if I hadn't come here. Truth, that is.

'That's down to my boy, my eldest, that's the one that living with me now. He said, "it's the only place – place I've heard people talking about." And I said "oh yeah". "Well, come down with me," and he brought me down here. This is my eldest boy. That's when Rosie's on the desk. You remember? "Yes, he can have a job," she said to me. I said thank you. Then he said, my boy said, "there y'are, dad." Yes, very good that was. Nice to talk about it now and again, you know what I mean? Is very nice to talk about it.

'I thought, I won't be here for long, will I?' Croak of laughter. 'But I'm glad I have. Bin a great help to me. Great help indeed it has, definitely, when I can get out, do a few gardens, or do me own, you know. Anyway, that's how it goes, innit?

'You're not gonna believe this, the happiest time in my life is when my grandmother and grandfather used to take us down to Clacton. Making sand castles, stupid things you do when you're a kid. That's the happiest time of my life, when I'm with them all, know what I mean? Me mother, me father, me grandfather and me grandmother. Not so much me grandfather, but he'd come with us, like, you know. There'd be me and me sister, and me mum and dad, all down in Clacton, all go together. And I miss that. Yeh. Don't seem to realise, do you, when it starts. Think "oh you're gonna last forever, be here for good." But you're not, are you?

'All we got is good mem'ries. Really good mem'ries. If I could be like that all the time, you know what I mean? But you can't. You begin to wonder where everybody's gorn to. You know what I mean?

'What's the time? Bugger me, is that three? I'm orf.'

Rose's story

Rose is 56, medium tall, quite thin. Her hair, once black, now greying, is pulled tightly back from her strong, high cheekboned face. She moves awkwardly, feet turned widely out, but determinedly and fast. Her face and voice are very flexible, sometimes full of emotion, sometimes deadpan, almost hieratic: a born story-teller.

I was born in East London, and I was born in 1942. I had three sisters and one brother. We all had good times, we had bad times as well.

When I was born, I was dumb. When I was two years of age, my mother took me to the hospital in Hackney, which is still there to this day. It was very difficult for me when I did start talking, because I wasn't pronouncing my words like I should have done, but people manage to know what I'm talking about, so to me that's all that worries me.

I had a beautiful childhood, I mean it had ups and downs, but I had stories to last me all my life. Like my Nan and my mum used to go down Roman Road every Saturday, and my grandfather was a carman by trade, he used to drive horse and cart. So this Saturday, he turned round and said to my Nan, "while you're down the Roman," he said, "could you get me a couple of pairs of socks," he said. So my Nan said "yeah, all right," she said. So her and mum goes off down the market. So my Nan saw a couple of her friends, so from one pub to the other they went, so of course by time she got down the market, she forgot what she'd got to get, and she got a pair of kippers for me grandfather's tea. So of course in they comes, my Nan rolling down the street, singing her head off.

So he turned round and said, "Madge, did you get me me socks," so she said "socks?" She said, "no," she said, "but I got you a nice pair of kippers." So he said "I can't wear bloody kippers on me feet, can I?"

And my Nan, when the air raids was on, she used to run out in the middle of the turning, she wouldn't go in the shelter, no, not her! She'd roll her sleeves up, "come down here and fight fair, you bastards, come down here!" My grandfather, he used to say "Mad, get in that bloody shelter." "Sod the bleeding shelter," she used to say. "I'm doing what I'm doing, you do what you're doing."

My stepfather was a very understanding man. As far as I'm concerned, my stepfather is my father. Because my own father walked out when I was 12 weeks old. My mum got married to my stepdad and had a child, I was about four, five years old. I didn't know my own father till I was 21. But as far as I knew, the dad that I grew up with was my dad.

My dad, my stepfather, he worked all the hours God almighty sent, every day of his life, rain, sleet, snow, sunshine, he would do any kind of work just so us children would have a good life. I'm not saying we were rich, because we wasn't. They used to deliver to Buckingham Palace, to the queen and all the top nobs. And this particular day, the driver went round this corner, bang, straight into a truck. My dad ended up with broken spine, 17 years he suffered and even though he was in a wheelchair, he still helped us girls as much as he could, in his own little way.

People used to say, wherever your dad is, you're with him, always up his backside as you might say. I'd come home from school, I'd be sitting at the

Rose in the garden at 42

street door waiting for Dad to turn the corner, he used to put his arms out, swing me round like, he would come into my room, he used to sit for hours and hours with me, doing my homework. And even when he was ill, and I was taken into hospital, I was feeling so down because I was told about my Addisons, and Dad managed to get up on crutches and he walked in through that door, and that was like giving me a new life. And I go over to the cemetery, and I still talk to him when I sit in my house. And sometimes when I'm sitting there, I can still see him sitting there. He's always there. I mean, I'm sitting here talking to you now, Pebs, he's with me. He's saying "what you crying for, silly moo? What you crying for?" He had a good sense of humour, he did, very good sense of humour.

Course, I didn't finish school. When I was the age of 14, I got knocked down by a 35-seater motor coach, and I was in a wheelchair for two years, and they didn't have the facilities at school for wheelchairs like they do today. And so my father taught me at home, so what I do know, which is not a lot, I've got Dad to thank. I started work at the age of 15, 16, I started work in me wheelchair, working for Lesney's toy factory.

It was my father got me to walk again. The hospital said I'd never walk again. My father was a determined man, I thank him for it now, I didn't then. "There's no such word as can't, not even in the dictionary," he used to say. "Dad, I cannot move." "How d'you know unless you try?" he used to say. "If you fall, you get up again, doncha?" And every day after he came home from work, and I come home from work, he started off an hour, it went on to two hours, to get me walking.

My mother, she's always been for my eldest sister and my youngest. She's never bin for me. I mean, when I had my Richard, Richard was in incubator and tubes and that, and my mother, she said to me "he'd be better off dead, don't you think?" I felt like hitting her, I really did, and I've never raised my hand to any of my parents. So she said, "you'll never manage him, the way he is." So I said "You don't know what I can do," I said. I said, "Dad managed me, didn't he, when I wasn't walking?" So my mother never came in the hospital to see me from then on.

Time I was in the hospital after the accident, I had my very first boyfriend, he was a porter in the hospital and his name was Kenny. We're still friends to this very day. Deep down, yes, deep down I love him. Cause there is a saying, no love is like the first love. We was going to get married, I was just turned 15. Kenny wanted us to get a flat and move in together. And my mother wouldn't hear of it. He turned round and said to me, "The way I love you I just can't bear to be without you," he said, "so it would be better if we go our separate ways," you know. But – I would still have had my Richard, naturally, but his name probably wouldn't have been Richard. And probably I would have had my own house, wouldn't have been in the situation I am now. You know, I don't know where I'm gonna be from one day to this. It's private landlord, see. My bathroom, ceiling's like *that* where the water's coming in, it's just hanging. I got no bannister on the stairs, I've got no doors on the rooms.

I've always been the unlucky one with love-life and that, except for Kenny, like. I mean, before I married Georgie, I was married before, and he was in and out of prisons, and he kicked me down iron staircase when I was pregnant, I lost the baby, so that split up. It was all right for first six months, then it started, prison and that. Robbery, non-payment of fines, things like that. And I thought to myself, well I'm still young, why should I put up with that life? So when he was in prison, I put up with it for three years, so I went in for the divorce on ground of desertion and beating me up. Then I was on me own for a long long time.

I had a flat, I had my dad living with me, not my stepfather, my own dad. I wouldn't call him Dad. I never called him Dad. I wouldn't. As far as I'm concerned, my dad that brought me up, he was my dad. I mean I never knew no other person as my dad, for 21 years I never even knew he existed, so I just couldn't call him Dad, Pebs, I just couldn't.

My dad, my stepfather, used to dine out on a Friday night, to have a drink in a pub. He met Georgie and they become friends and one Saturday Georgie asked me if I would like to go to a show. I decided to go, and then a year later we was married. My husband and I are much better acquainted now than what we was when we was living together. I used to dislike him coming home drunk, belting me, belting the child, so I packed a few bits for me and Richard and walked out and I've bin on my own ever since with Richard.

We ended up in a bed & breakfast, we got out the bed & breakfast and had temporary accommodation. When we was offered another house to live in, Richard asked me if I would think of taking his dad back, I tried it, it only lasted six months. He was violent to Richard, not to me, to Richard. But as time went on we got friendly again.

And seven years ago I heard that I have got an incredible disease, which is called Addisons Disease. I have been told by the hospital every time I go that I have deteriorated, but I just take it with a pinch of salt. But I do get days that, you know... But I think to myself, well, thank God I'm here today, like, and I thank God for another day, like, you know. That's the way I look at it. Now, I've got that I just if I wake up tomorrow, I think "thank God," and if I don't I don't. That's the way I look at it, Pebs.

I mean I know for a fact that if any time I was very ill and I was in hospital and that, people down here would come and see me, you know what I mean, I've got all my friends down here, that's why I love coming down here. I feel that the Friary has backed me up all the way, and I mean this house is my second home, that's the only way I can put it, Pebs, it's my second home. Richard was five years old when I first used to come to this place. And at the moment I am sitting here with a friend of mine called Pebbles and told her this story because it's the story of my life.

Now, my mother-in-law, she was a lovely woman, she was. She was 100 on 10th October, she died on 9th, so she never got the telegram from the Queen. My mother-in-law was due to spend a few weeks with me and Georgie, like, and she fell ill. I said to Georgie I said, "I'll phone to see how Mum is." So Richard turned round and said, "Mum," he said, "what's the matter with Nanny Barton? She ain't here." So I said "I know she ain't here, she's in North Wales." So he said, "no," he said, "she's gone to heaven." So I said to him, "you bleeder," I said, "don't you ever talk about your Nanny like that." I phoned my brother-in-law, I said, "can I speak to your mum?" So he said to me, "I'm afraid you can"t," he said, "Mum died this afternoon." My Richard knew.

My Nan, she was Romany. She brought me up. When my mum and my own father split up, like, before she met my dad that I call my dad, she used to go to work and my Nan used to look after us. And I knew my Derek was in trouble, even before he come and told me. I don't know whether we got it from our Nan or not.

My eldest sister's boy, he was going to Switzerland. So I says to my sister, I said "Ive," I said, "I hope he misses the plane." So the phone rang, so it was John. So his mum said, "why, you're going to be late getting to Switzerland." So he said, "no, the plane I should've been on crashed." And there was no survivors. And I dreamt that. That's why I don't like, if I go into a deep sleep, deeply deeply dream, whatever I dream comes true. It's frightening, cause it always comes true.

And me and Derek, we're more closer than any of the other children, like. He's like my twin. Whether we can do it now, I don't know, but normally if he has toothache, I have toothache, we've got that kind of thing going between us.

My Derek, I miss him terribly. My Derek and me, we had the same dad but different mums, like, you know. We were same age, though, same birthday. He used to be a boxer, he's got cups for boxing. And course Derek's had tragedies, and lost his son, and he got married to Chrissie, which is a lovely girl. See, my Derek, he's a silly boy really to hisself. I mean he was going straight, 13 years my Chrissie got him out of trouble, and then I don't know what snapped, I mean even when he lost Jason he picked himself up again, but something just turned, and he's just gone back to the way he was. I mean he's in prison now for beating up his daughter, and I don't know what's turned him again.

Regular job – that's something I can never get, cos of my illness. Cos I had a beautiful job. I started off in Tesco's as a shelf-filler, and by the time I had my illness, I was supervisor. But every time I go to the hospital, I say, "look can I get a job, I'm fed up with being the way I am." So he says to me, "don't forget, Rosie, you're deteriorating every day," he said, "and not only that," he said, "you could end up in hospital for three or four months at a time," he said, "so no employer would stand it," he said. If I could get a job, obviously wouldn't have to rely on Social so much. I mean, I'm not being big or anything, but I done a course in Steps and I passed that, and I've got CVs of what I've done and everything, so I could get a proper job.

I mean, I enjoy doing the *Issue*. You get to meet all different kinds of people, and they stand there, some of them, and tells you jokes, you know. If they give you a two pound coin, I always say to them, "hang on, madam, sir, and I'll give you" – and they say to me, "that's for you," like, you know. Not only that, but sometimes, Richard might say to me, "Mum, can you afford to buy me a packet fags, I'll give the money back to you Monday." Then I'll do it, cause I've got money.

Sometimes I don't finish the *Issue* not till seven o'clock, and by time I get home, I'm just whacked. It's travelling backwards and forwards, cos go to Kings Cross, then you go to your pitch, then you've go back to Kings Cross to get more magazines, cos you're frightened to take too many case you don't sell them. I'd rather get me magazines that I know I can sell and go back and get more, rather than buy 50 or 60 at a time and then I've ended up with 30 or 40 of them left, like, you know what I mean?

It's just – I would like to do a regular job. I'd like to work with disabled children. They're so lovable, you know. I mean all children are lovely, but handicapped children, they've just got that special something.

I do see myself as strong. My dad give me that. How I am now is all down to my dad. It was only my dad's confidence that got me to walk again. It made me feel stronger in meself. I think that is why when Dad ended up in a wheelchair I started taking him out, cos he done it for me.

My Richard's pushed him in his wheelchair. My Richard was the only one could understand what my dad was saying. My mum used to say things, "I dunno what he wants, I wish he could bleeding talk," she said. So Richard said to her, "I'll get him to tell you what he wants." So this particular day, Richard, he touched his hand, so he said, "Grandad, look at me." My dad looked straight at him. So he said, "Grandad, if you want a cup of tea," he said, "blink your eyes once. See? If you want to go to the toilet, blink them twice. If you want to go in a different room," he said, "blink four times." My dad done it, he done that right to the day he died.

And I mean it might sound silly, but my aim is I wanna be here to see my Richard turn into a nice lad, to get married, have a fam'ly of his own, and be like anybody else in the world. I don't think that's too much to ask, Pebs. Once I can see that, then I don't care if I die or not, you know what I'm saying? I've had that attitude ever since I had the Addisons. I'm gonna be here to see my Richard grown up and married. I'm gonna be here to see my Richard grown up and married. I mean whatever Richard does, I wish him luck in doing it, Pebs.

But I said to him, I said, "son," I said, "just be careful." So he said "what you mean, be careful?" "With *that,*" I said. "Don't you dare overdose." I said. "It's no good saying you won't, son," I said "you might come to a time when you want it desperately, you'll go and get some, you smoke it all at once and bang, you're not here any longer." So he said to me, "I suppose you're right," so I said "I know I'm right." So his dad turned round and said "of course your mother's right."

If that's the way he chooses to live, it's up to him, Pebs. I mean he's a man now, he's 18. As my dad used to say. "You made your bed, you lay on it. We'll help you as much as we can, but the rest is up to you. We can't tell you what to do, it's up to you in the long run what you do." Which is right, Pebs, innit?

Richard said last night, he wants to get a car, he wants to do this and he wants to do that. And I turned round and said to him, "well if you want to do all that, son, get up off your bloody backside and do it! Cos no one else is gonna do it for you." So Georgie turned round and said, "go and sign on at the Labour," he said. "Isn't it better," he said, "to earn your money for your things than to rely on other people, like the State and that? You get £74 a week," he said, "where if you got a job you could be earning £174 a week," he said. Which is right, really, Pebs. Georgie said, "when you"ve got something you've got to stay at it and stay at it and stay at it," he said. "I've done it for 75 years," he said, "so I know."

But, anyway. That's me, gel!

Trevor's story

Trevor is quite tall, strongly built. His voice, like his movements, is quick and abrupt; his sentences come in swift hammer-blows – yet not aggressively. His face is very alive, with a flashing smile; he looks straight at whoever he's talking to, alert and interested.

My name is Trevor Tull, I'm 22, I've lived in Plaistow most of my life, but when I was little I moved to Canning Town. I lived there for 11 years, and now I'm back at Plaistow.

I went to Eastleigh Community School, and St Luke's and New City when I was younger. I had to go to New City cause I was dyslexic. They helped me with my reading and writing. Home was okay. My little sister's not around any more. My little brother's a pain in the backside but that's life. We was always round my Nan's house, but now they're not around, so I don't go round to fam'ly, I go round to my friend's house.

Nan? She's lovely. That's why I'm working with elderly people, cause when she was alive she was – like she was paralysed down one side. But she was the only one that ever used to be able to get me to sleep. My mum used to walk the streets with me, three o'clock in the morning, trying to get me to sleep. But then she took me round to my Nan and my Nan just laid me like acrost her, and I was asleep within a second. I was round there near enough every single day, before I went to school, after I went to school, most weekends. Me and me mum and me brother more or less lived with me Nan for about two years, because the house above us, they had a flood, it all come through the roof, it ruined everything, two and a half grand's worth of stuff it ruined. And I was very ill through it all and everything, that's why I've got asthma now, partly, partly it's people smoking around me, hate that stuff, stinks, specially on me clothes.

I miss them badly, you know, I've never bin able to get used to them not being around, my grandparents and my little sister. Never from that day to this day. But I've got to do that, somehow. Little sister? Cot death. I was five years old when it happened. Meant a lot to me. Very much. Thing that upsets me more than anything, I never got properly to say goodbye to her. That's maybe why I'm like I am, I always like cry sometimes when I talk about her, you know.

My Nan's bin dead 11 to 12 years, Grandad's bin dead I think about nine years to ten years. Loving, they were. They help you. See, me Nan and my Grandad used to – like they got on with this policeman, he always used to go round to see me Grandad and Nan and see how they were and everything. They got friends next door, they were always in me Nan's house – West Indian people. They always used to see how my Nan and Grandad were if me mum weren't there. It's lovely.

Just miss the fam'ly not being together. I live with my mum. I was close to her when I was little. Not so much now. I used to get called mummy's little boy! But not no more. Kind of grown up a bit. There's just me and my brother then my little sister. And my aunts, my uncle – my uncle lives in Kent.

Me other Nan and Grandad, like me dad's mum and dad, they live in Kent, on a barge – Rosie and Jim boat, got exactly the same as that. It's lovely. I was the first person on the boat, with me Grandad, when we collected it, went through all the locks and everything. Blinding.

School was ok. I used to get picked on a lot. Cause I wouldn't fight back. And then one day I had a fight and since that no one's touched me. Didn't want to fight. But there was one time my cousin, one of my cousins that I went to school with, he in ways pushed me into a fight, because my brother was getting picked on. And I was standing there watching it, and then me cousin pushed me into it, so I had a fight with him. People laid off me after that, yuh. Eastleigh school and Cumberland fight a lot, things happen in them places, so you have to fight back in ways. But I never wanted to fight. Cos if you beat one person, then they're gonna go and get more people on to you. So I just kept meself to meself. But I still got picked on. Cos I was quiet, and wouldn't answer back to anybody, until one day I just had enough, and had a fight.

Me? sport mad. See I studied football for 12, 14 years, maybe longer, I know near enough everything about football that there is. I just watch it left right and centre, to understand more what's going on. I just love it. I'm good in goal, good in defence, good attacker. I used to play for Sunday team, semi-pro, but all split up and everything. Like to be a pro – yuh. That was my dream. That was a dream that never come true for me, to become a professional footballer. Plus where I was at school I never got the chance to prove meself to anybody. They always used to leave me as sub and everything. But I was the main one that turned up for every training game. The teacher just had his favourites, like the normal teachers, and I weren't one of them. Cos there was players better than me in our year but I never got the chance to prove myself against them. You know. Don't play now. I wisht I could. There is adult teams, but I just got to go round ask them. Cause I live near Memorial Park, and there's teams over there, it's just getting to the Away games I can't.

I got medals for football, swimming, horse riding. Yuh. It was my cousin that got us into it, me and my brother. In North Woolwich there used to be a place, it's gone to North Beckton now. There's horses down there, and I used to ride them down there.

Dad drives a lorry. Me mum is going for jobs, to do similar to what I'm doing, with the elderly people. But she's going into things like stroke and everything. She's used to that, cos she was little girl when me Nan had her stroke. I've always loved elderly people, and felt I wanted to do something for them, so done this. All these things you can find out about the olden days and what they were like and that. See, when my mum's dad was alive, I used to sit round there listening to him tell me about the olden days. See how different it is from then to now. You used to be able to leave your doors wide open in them days. Prob'ly if you done that now you'd go back and the house would be emptied!

Me mum and dad worry a lot, about me and my brother. Because the stuff that's bin happening around, like people getting stabbed and stuff like that. It's hard, living here. Because things now is harder to get, like jobs, houses, stuff like that. You know. Maybe in the year 2000 everything's gonna go wrong, like they've bin saying. The bug, computer bugs and all that. Just gonna muck up, I reckon.

See, if I had a lot of money, I'd like to go to a different country, like Italy or New Zealand or something like that. I know I shouldn't, but in different places you get thought of, I reckon, in other countries. Because the tax in this country, for a man to own his own business on a lorry, it's costing five and half thousand, yuh? In France, their tax is 385 pound. It's just diabolical, why they have to raise our tax two, maybe three times more than any other country. Money in this country, it's diabolical. Because, see – where we're united with other countries for the EU, it's gonna be twice as worse. Because you have to pay more tax on the EU, don't you? So... I just wanna get some money behind me and leave this country.

I'm also like a qualified mechanic by trade. So if I couldn't get a job out in another country working with the elderly, I could go as a mechanic. Or I could go as an actor, see. I got a diploma in acting. BTech First, Performing Arts. 1991. I started school when I was eight, I left in '93. I went straight to New Vic to do acting in '93. In '94 I went to East Ham college to do mechanics. I've bin to college for about seven to eight years, and so far I got two grades behind me, and no one's wanted to give me a job out there. Specially for mechanics. Cos you need the experience. So I thought fair enough, that's when I started here, Helping Hands. Yep.

See, I always enjoyed acting, and I thought I'll give it a go. I done *Momo*, *Life in the City*, there was another two. But I enjoyed it. I met different people in that way. And I know how to build a stage up, from bottom to top. But like I

Lost. I'm lost. It's like Spaghetti Junction, so many possibilities, which road do I take? Which junction will get me where I want to go to? Where do I want to go to? I don't know, I don't have the answers.

Who does have the answers? I don't know. Who do I ask? So many questions but no answers. Spaghetti Junction, which exit do I take? How do I get off this roundabout? I'm going round and round in circles. I wish someone would help me. I'm getting dizzy, going round and round.

Spaghetti Junction. I can't read the signposts. I need someone to read them for me. A navigator, that's what I need.

Who will be my navigator? Who will read the signposts? I don't know. More questions, still no answers. Life is full of questions without answers.

A map! That's it, I need a map! Where can I get a map? Another question. Still no answers. I need to think, I need to work it out. Work out the route. Where the end is. But what route? Where do I want to end up? Oh no! Another set of questions. Who has the answers? Not me, that's sure.

I want to scream. Going round and round. I open my mouth but no sound comes out.

I'm lost, Spaghetti Junction, getting dizzy, fading fast, I need help. I can't find my way.

Jason

never followed the acting up, cos once they didn't want me in the BTech National, in Performing Arts, I didn't know whether I'd be able to go any further. I just went straight to mechanics. Cos like me uncle, he's a qualified mechanic, and my two cousins, they're like qualified mechanics. It's hard, my uncle not living round here. He rebuilds cars, from scratch, just the shells. Got three American lorries, as well.

I used to work agencies and stuff like that. I wanted a full time job, to get money and go out and buy myself stuff. But it's hard at the moment for anybody my age. Me brother's got a job, but he knew the people he's working for, you know? He's a qualified chef. It's getting the experience. That's why I never got a job as a mechanic, because I haven't got the experience. But when I first started going for college, you had to have the qualifications. See, I know what I'm doing when I'm working on cars, it's just that I don't wanna mess it up because I'm messing with a person's life there. When you're working on a car, you're messing with people's lives, really.

I should get a job once my police chit comes through. I got a clean record left right and centre, I know that for a fact. It's just that I've got to prove it. Cause you're dealing with the elderly. If you get a two-year probation and you don't do nothing in them two years, your record's clean. But as soon as you do something in them two years, you're stuck for life.

Best thing that could happen? West Ham to win the European Cup, the Champions Cup, the FA Cup and the Worthington Cup all at once, me to win the National Lottery. I'd give some of it to my mum and dad, Nan and Grandad, my two uncles, my brother, and take my brother, most of my friends on holiday. Bahamas, or Trinidad, places like that. I'd take friends on holiday with me. And I'd be gone. If I won the Lottery tomorrow I'd be gone. Find work. Cause I know for a fact I've got mechanical behind me, but if I never got a job I'd leave this country and go somewhere else and find a job. See, I've got a best girl friend, and a best boy friend. But my best mate who's the boy, he's moved up to Yarmouth. I used to be with him every single day, when he finished work he'd come round for me or vice versa. Girls didn't like it. Because I know that most men do this, but we was always down the pub or out fishing, stuff like that, but now I can't do that with him, cause he lives down Yarmouth and I live down here. I've bin down there a few times with him, to stay, it's lovely down there. Blinding. His mum and dad live down there. Cos they used to live round here, in Corporation Street, but they moved, cause they wanted somewhere better. Yarmouth, Clacton, I'd love to live – really.

Happiest time? Oh, holding FA Cup. 1980, when West Ham won the FA Cup against Arsenal. I was three. My mum took me when they paraded the Cup round Upton Park. I used to live in Plaistow Road, so I went over to there. Blinding. One of the best things that ever happened to me. I got photos indoors to prove it, as well. I was a lucky person then.

Daphne's story

Daphne is small and indomitable, possessed of her own irreverent humour. Her hair is long, fair and fine, pulled hard back from her round, determined face into a bun or down her back. Fifty-five years old, she's an East Ender, born and bred.

'I'll always maintain I had a privileged childhood. There wasn't much money, but if it's care and love, I had it.

'My uncle was mayor of Walthamstow. We used to go up to every museum – he had a pass, you see. By the time I was about 10 I'd seen everywhere. I was never bored – when it wasn't trips, it was Wanstead Flats for a picnic, or Wanstead Park, tiddling – we had our tins with strings over the tops. Even if on Sunday it was pouring with rain, my mum would build us a tent indoors and make teacakes, we'd all have them under the tent, together. There were bad times, I suppose, but so many good times that you don't think how bad the bad times were.'

But Daphne and Pat got scarlet fever. 'My mum couldn't see us. I had to spend my fifth birthday in hospital – there was one nurse, she was really hateful. I've never forgotten her face, and I never will.' But the night nurse – 'she was lovely. I'll never forget her face. On the way home – it was November, very foggy, but I didn't care, the sun was shining for me.

'Our Christmasses were totally magic. Money was very scarce, we didn't ask for anything, we were happy with what we got. We always spent Christmas at my aunt's, two streets away. We used to run through the streets,' looking up at the street lamps through the snow. Magic.

Daphne's uncle, in a wheelchair: 'he had rheumatoid arthritis, and he was an amazing man. I looked on him as father in a way, cos I was totally disciplined by him. But he was a very very clever man. While his hands were okay, he used to make all our clothes for us, and he made us a beautiful dolls house. His courage was absolutely second to none.

'One time, my mum and uncle managed to take him up the pub, and they come back, absolutely falling about with laughter, and he'd lost his teeth in the gutter, and they had to go out next day and look for them. And they wheeled him up the path that night, and he was going "my teef!" When he died I was devastated, I was about 15 or 16 I think.

'My father just left when I was eight months old. I don't remember him, and I wasn't bothered, because I thought if anyone can do that, they're not worth bothering about. But I would've liked my mum to have had somebody, because her whole life was focused on us, and I thought she deserved something much better. My mum worked too hard for us. It used to worry me, even though I was a kid. She did housework, five bob a morning. Buses she couldn't afford, so she would walk – well, run, virtually. She never got anything off my father. There was no child benefit – what we had was what she got. We never went without. It was all credit to my mum. Oh, she was a lovely person. She had an absolutely crackshot sense of humour, and she had a great brain on her. You'd have to get up early to get over her, in the morning, I tell you.

'But she was a very forthcoming person, nobody would stripe her for anything, she would stand up for herself, which was something I couldn't do. I've learnt how to now. But loads of people liked her, you know? And nobody more than I did. And I respected her, and there was a lot of love there. Although maybe sometimes I might not have shown it, I might have been a little bit offhand – but people are like that, it doesn't mean you think any the less of a person. We had our ups and downs – especially when I took home my spotty boyfriend. She went "oh my god," she said, "oh my god." I had my first boyfriend at six years old, dirty little devil, he was. It was just to say you'd got a boy in tow. He could look like a dog, it didn't matter. Some of them did look like dogs.

'They were golden days – doesn't mean they always run smoothly – but the bad bits weren't that bad. Whatever I went through, maybe at school, I always knew she was there when I got home. Those were really happy days.'

At five, Daphne started dancing. 'I had flat feet. Goes with me flat head, dunnit? And the doctor thought that if I went somewhere where I could point my feet, it would give me strength in me feet. It wasn't cheap, because you had to pay for these things. I took to it like a duck to water, and then we got the shows and everything, which were hard work. It was like from school work you went straight on to doing your training. The opening nights were scarey, really frightening. First time I did an opening night, I got this round of applause, I nearly had heart attack. I was about eight, and I was absolutely petrified, but – thing is, once you step out there, you're just doing what you're doing. After that first time, I concentrated on what I'd learnt, what I had to do. I was doing acrobatics and ballet and tap. I liked tap. I'll always remember that smell of the make-up – wouldn't mind some of that now, wouldn't half cover a lot! Just special sort of smell which you associate with that sort of thing.

'As I got older, I was offered a job as a choreographer in America. I wasn't ready for it. I knew I wasn't going to make a career of it. For me, it's for fun. That's enough. It's having a life that suits you. And America, it was like the moon. I've no regrets, because I had my chance and if I didn't take it, that was my choice.

'It's just being somebody else and not being yourself, I suppose. One costume I really got attached to was the one that I did my exam in, it was blue and black. And I was kind of sneered at, because I was an amateur and I was going against all these professionals, and they said, "oh, look at you, you'll never get any-where," and all this. And I went and passed and I was so thrilled. I thought – you know – I'm not gonna let them put me down – but I didn't think I would pass.

'And we used to go to the seaside, I did me routine on the sand, you know you can't do much on the pebbled beach at Brighton, which I tried hard enough, I tell you. They were great times. And I'd do it all over again. Cos there – there's a feeling that I can't describe about what it was like when I was younger.

'I went to Godwin Junior, which I loved. I could read fluently before I started school, and I could write a bit. When we had a reading lesson, they let me go up to the library and select what I liked for myself, for 10 year-olds. I could handle something harder, they knew I could. I loved it.'

But, 'my secondary school – it was awful from day one and I left at 14.

You know, until I left, I didn't realise what a cruel person my head teacher was. I was dead scared. If you did anything wrong, including at weekends, you were given the cane, you were given a hell of a time. It was such a shock

The pond on Wanstead Flats

– they were so nice at my Junior school. When you're bullied... I didn't want to worry Mum. That's why at 14 I eventually left – I told her I can't do this any more. We had a long talk. As soon as I was 15, I got a job. I was still doing school work at home up to then.

'I could've learnt a lot more had they been different. Really you were frightened to do anything at all. I would've liked to have gone to university. But they blocked out anything like that. I've always had good jobs, but I could've done something – it wasn't what I could've done. From the age of nine, I only ever wanted to be a mum, I didn't particularly want to get married. As I got older, I would have liked to have been a barrister, cos I'm interested in criminal law. I can imagine that some of it is pretty hairy, but – it was just something I liked. But I was a lot older, and financially I couldn't have done it anyway.

'When I was about 25 I think, 26, I was a partner in a business, buying and selling cars. He was my fiancé, who taught me how to drive. *Never* let your loved one teach you how to drive. We had this car, it was a pig, it wouldn't go for anybody but him, it really wouldn't. We ended up selling that, we towed it up to this bloke who said he'd buy it without even driving it. We thought we was on to a winner there, weren't we. We had another one, it was like the Flintstones, you put your foot down, and you could feel the road. Oh, we had some great motors, we did.

'It was before I married. I split up with him, I couldn't cope with his behaviour. Obsessive behaviour, where he sat outside my house all night, cos he thought I was seeing somebody else. And he'd accuse people of having a relationship with me. I nearly died when he accused the postman – I mean, you should have seen that postman. I was really upset when we split up. But – oh, after a year or so, I thought, I'm free. It took me about a year to realise he wasn't watching me.'

But that was later. 'First job was best. I worked in a brewery. I was there for six years, I really liked it. £3 5/4d a week, I earned, I was so proud of it. It was a dingey office, there was rats, I didn't care, I was just happy to be there.' Then, a job at the GLC. 'I saw a job advertised in the paper, only those with A' and O' levels need apply – as usual. I didn't have either. So I told them, "Oh yes, I've got A' level cookery and O' level woodwork, how's that going to help me fill a tax form out? I can read and write, surely that's what's needed."' Daphne was there three years. Then an agency job, then the last job, the worst: 'that was a life sentence, that was.'

But it was good to earn. 'You paid your mum, and you bought your clothes. There was a little clothes shop next door. They got to know me. If there was a jumper – maybe £5 – they'd say "never mind, dear, pay us £1 a week." But I never would take it, not till I'd paid it all. I never would get into debt.'

Finally, Daphne married. 'He beat me up all the time. I had to get out, or he'd kill me. He was very quiet and unassuming, it was only afterwards he started. Terrible mistake, I made. God, I was full of them in those days. And – you know, when I left him, it was – oh, could've done cartwheels down the street! I mean, he destroyed everything I had. Basically, I was frightened of him, very frightened. He'd just come at me and wallop, I'd be on the floor. I'd go into a room, I'd let him go in first, in case he attacked me. I didn't know what violence was like when I was a kid, so to get it at the age of 30 – it made me feel ill.

'My mum knew. I thought she didn't, you know, I was trying to hide it. And she kept saying, "why don't you leave him," and I said "I'm going to," I said. And I walked out with just a carrier bag, and couldn't have been happier. But after that, I thought, I don't want anybody else. I didn't want to get in that situation again.

'It was about three years before I met anybody else. And I was absolutely stunned. I'd been going out with him for a week, and I thought, "he hasn't hit me yet, why hasn't he hit me?" He couldn't understand what was wrong with me. And I remember telling him. He was sitting there crying, he said, "I can't believe it," he said, "I'll never hurt you." I thought to myself, it's too late now, the damage is done. He never did did hurt me. But I finished that relationship. These people leave a legacy, and you never feel you ever want to be part of a relationship again.'

Daphne's been out of work 'about 15, 16 years. The last one – that was another goodbye that I enjoyed. I said, "I'd rather be in the gutter than work here for you!" and that's where I've landed, in the gutter! I think that was the one that made me stand up for myself a lot, you know. Being there for 12 years, and realising just what they were all about, it really made me think, nobody's going to take advantage of me any more. It was the sort of place that if your face fitted, you was okay. If you did exactly what you were told, which – I found it hard – you were okay.

'But they done the dirty on me because they asked me to help out in another office, and I said I would – we'd had a strike, it was going on for weeks. And when I went back to my office, they'd given my job to someone else. And I went into one about it. Nobody would tell me why they done it. I mean, I'd worked seven years in that job, and I'd done all right, used to take stuff home and work on it. I don't know why they did it.

'So I thought well, I'll turn the tables, and I used to roll in at ten o'clock, half past ten, and I started, you know, playing up. I was desperately unhappy. I didn't want to do that, it was just – kind of getting my own back. I went to the union, and it was hopeless, he didn't want to know. I got ill then. It was really telling on me, I was really unhappy. And they started sending me letters saying that if you don't come back to work, we'll dismiss you. And I kept having to go back, and meetings and what-not. And at last I left. Longest lunch hour in history. It was a Tuesday. I walked out lunch time and never been back.

'But you see it was awkward, because I'd never ever been on the dole. I didn't know what it was like. I was in my early 40s, 39? So I had to go down there, and they said "how comes you lost your job after all this time?" Anyway, they said they're not going to give me any dole money for three months, because they said I was dismissed through misconduct. And I said, "that is not true." She said, "I know it isn't," she said. And I said, "but I'm not gonna get another job. How am I ever gonna find work if they're saying that?"

'And I never did. I never ever did get another job. I can only assume that the references put them off. It was frustrating, you see, most of my jobs have been figure-work – not computers, all in your head. And they just couldn't accept it, that I could just run off a row of figures and get it right. And so somewhere along the line, it kind of got a bit lost.

'I mean, when I got my dole payment eventually, £23 a week, I thought what am I going to do on this? And it was a nightmare. So I tried to find something else, but I couldn't get it. After all those years of working, and all the experience I gained, I couldn't get anything. And that's why I started ringing round, I thought anything's better than nothing. And I found a job in the supermarket, and that was – oh, they were mean, they were really mean. Rotten backless chairs, they had. We used to have a bloke come in every Monday morning, with a £20 note, for a packet of chewing gum. I said, "what, after your bus fare?" I said, "we ain't even got that in the float." Anyway, I left there, I couldn't wait. First and last time in a supermarket, didn't last that long. Thought I was doing all right there, as well, but – you know. And I tried again, and just nothing. I was never lucky enough to moonlight, I've never been able to do it. I'd be scared. But it was hard, cos there was Mum on a pension, and there was me. Lived together since I left my husband.

'I gave up after about five years. They kept getting on to me, "why haven't you got a job?" And I said, "well, it's obvious, there's so many people out of work." I couldn't believe that I would never be working. But that's actually how it ended up. I mean I wasn't stupid, I wasn't slow, I can write and read, I've done lots of jobs, and I couldn't believe that I just couldn't get anything. And well, that was that.

'And then of course Mum got ill, and there was no way I would have gone to work. But now, the DSS've said I might have to go for a medical, and I'm panicking, because it's at Kings Cross or somewhere, and the thought of going up there just screws me up. So I've written that on the form, I have panic attacks. And I do. I'm terrified of getting on the train.

'When my mum was ill, I thought now you've got to go out. Was like it when I was working, just had to get on with it. I remember getting to Stratford, I was working at the Town Hall, I walked halfway and I just stood, I couldn't go forward and I couldn't go backward, I didn't know which way to turn. I ended up, I made myself go in, but I felt terrible all day.

'I don't know what brought it on. I can remember very clearly, I was in my first job, it was a Friday, I got paid, I was happy, happy home life, got a nice boyfriend and all this. I had it all. And I was going out with my mum at Stratford. And I got down there, there's a butcher's shop there, and I was walking past the butcher's shop and I just froze. And that was it, my life changed. I just stopped and I just froze. And it seemed like everybody was coming up to me, like crowds of people all around – but they weren't. All their faces seemed to be right on mine. I didn't know where I was. And my mum took me home and I never went outside for a year.

'Had to leave that job. I couldn't even open the door and look out into the garden. It was my sister, she made me open the door, then put my foot out on the step, it took me a year to get out the house. Once I'd got my confidence back, no stopping me. I started going to dance halls and that, couldn't believe I was doing it. The first time I said "there's so many people" – the second time, I was there all blooming night.

'I think it's about not being in control. I was all right when I used to drive myself. But it's a horrible thing, because it stops you doing so much. Not to be able to go anywhere, not to be confident. I've never been abroad, for the same reason. And I find it embarrassing, because I don't tell anybody. Well, I have today, it's the first time. I can stomp round the corner, go to the shops, I always say I'm quite happy pottering about, but sometimes – when I think what I've missed out on...

'My mum, three years ago she died. She got some kind of ache in her side, then this sort of tingling, in her fingers, and I said right, to the doctor's. She wouldn't have it. Six months I was going on at her, to do it. And then she had the stroke.

'On Sundays we'd put the dinner in and go round the pub, she wasn't a drinker, one sherry, but she enjoyed it. Then we'd go home and have our dinner. I was always cooking, and she said "why don't you have a break?" but I said no, I loved it. But Saturday I used to get a Chinese, and we'd put a video on, and have a laugh with that and have a little sherry indoors, and it was nice. When I get down, I try to think of that.

'I'm still so guilty. All this time. I keep thinking, did I say something horrible, did I do this – I just can't help it. If I'd've insisted she went to the doctor, would it have bin different? But we were both the same, stubborn as mules. In build my sister is like her, and I'm like my dad. He used to like dancing on the stage, getting up and making a fool of himself, like me.

'Julian, he used to come over and see her, we'd known each other for years. When she died, he thought it would be a good idea to get me out the house. Cos I was welded in there. And then I got into a routine – so you had a reason to get up, you had a reason for doing something. So I'm really grateful for this – I mean, I might whinge now and again, but that's part of it, isn't it? But it gives me something to say, I'm going to work tomorrow, be doing this and doing that. It gives you something to think about, cos you're just all the time thinking about one thing.

'I mean, if I'd've bin married, with a family, they'd have bin left and I'd've gone back to her. There'd be no question about that. Whenever I went out, which was rare, I was always worried. She would always try and do things. She was so active, and she wasn't used to being like that, and I could understand that. But I'd do it again. Nothing would stop me. She is my mum, and you don't walk away. I mean she looked after me, my god, why shouldn't I do the same? And through my broken relationships, she nursed me through that. All my tantrums, cos things didn't go right. It's not that you owe somebody something, it's just that you want to do it.

'My childhood, it was really special. But there was this school holiday I went on. My sister had bin really ill. They thought she could recuperate. Sussex. That's why I don't like Sussex. Ended up with a wicked woman for a fortnight. Terrible. Never left my mum's side after that. You see, I was never ill-treated until I met this woman, and I couldn't believe it.

'She told me I'd never see my mum again. I was only eight. And she locked us in the house. We couldn't get out. She was the one kicked me hands off the breakwater. There was a river running where I was trying to learn to swim, I was clinging on, she just kicked my hands away. We used to count the days till we was coming home. And when we got home, our house had a bay window, I kept looking, I said "she's not coming to get us, is she? She's not going to take us back?" A wicked, evil woman.

'You see, I think they know when they can pick on somebody who won't answer back. When you're a child, that patterns your life, doesn't it? That patterns things. I wish I'd've bin a bit more forceful. But I suppose when you're at school, you feel you can't, because they're in charge, aren't they? But I think that's why I'm a bit like I am today, where I'll stand up to people. At last.'

John's story

John's small, wiry, quick-moving, very active. He and big Alan work together at Helping Hands, out and about most of the time. He speaks like he moves, quickly and emphatically. Hair's beginning to grey. He has a mind of his own. Nothing seems dull for John.

'I just done a moving job, you know, for an old lady. First of all it was a cupboard she wanted out, then she wanted a wireless taken out, then she wanted two eiderdowns taken out, then had to bring the bed downstairs, I suppose it's her husband's coming out of hospital, you know, she hasn't got nobody to do it.

So we lifted the bed down, and I said to Alan, "just slide it down the stairs!" So we slid it down the stairs! And she's a nice, well, it was a coloured lady. She said, "it's not heavy." I thought "heavy enough!" So we phoned the hot-line for her, take away the rubbish, and said "you want anything else done?" You got to see the size of the beds, though! Big! I reckon there's three lays in those beds!

'Then we done a garden, Monday and Tuesday, and we phoned the hot line for her. We had 16 bags out of this woman's garden! Then she wanted her front done! Oh, we done some gardens, we have, done some gardens.

'I used to, like, wood, just stacking. Since I've bin at school. When it come out the machine, used to come through planed, and they used to have so many on a barrer, and fork-lift used to come in and load it when the lorries come in. I was down Silvertown. Round the back there, I was there two years, and they shut down. You could do five days a week if you wanted to, or you could do seven days a week, but sometimes, you know, I thought you won't get no chance yourself, really, with yourself. So then I worked down Barking. There was a yard where they used to make the powder and that, washing-up stuff, used to work down there, woodyard down there.

'Christmas time used to be like – the woman used to do us a spread, lights, Christmas tree, chains, the lot. Put cans of beer on the table, and cakes, sandwiches, everything. And we put, I think it was a pound each, when she went out the room, we all said we'd put a pound, and get her something for doing all this. Well, I'll never forget this. We all put a pound each, and this bloke, he wouldn't put a pound down. Never forget that.

'Used to be – there's flats now where it used to be, along Barking Road, used to be a woodyard there. That's where I worked, oh, can't remember, few years. Sometimes I was feeding machines up, and I loved that. If the stuff's wet you

John and big Alan

gotta watch your hands, because you can see the rollers, taking the water off, if it turned quick, you could jam your hands. And there used to be conveyor belts coming down, and they used to put it from outside, down the rollers. Oh, it was lovely job. If it's not come out properly, you'd throw it on the side, you'd pick it up after, they'd cut it up for something else. As I say, used to do everything, you know, go on all the machines and everything. No, I think that was the best job I had, wood. Smell of it. Had a nice guv'nor.

'And night work, it was like a conveyor, coming out the wall, and lorries used to back on to them, and the people downstairs, they used to, like, pass the papers up to you, the driver used to say how many bundles he wanted on – lovely job. Sometimes you're waiting there for about half hour, hour, before the next lot comes up. Sometimes, just after one's gone another lorry used to come in. And then the first night I was there, I got a lift home, I didn't hardly know the bloke! Yeah, wasn't bad, they all worked together, like I thought oh, this is lovely job, you know. I think I was there about two nights, and that was it, they didn't want me any more. That was after the woodyards. That was three woodyards I worked for.

'I had some lovely jobs, though. They said, that one at Canning Town, they was gonna run a road through there. But it looks like they haven't done a thing. There used to be coloured blokes working on there. And there used to be a canteen, like a van, if you wanted a roll or something. And then after it was all shut down, somebody burnt the office down! For shutting it down! They ain't done nothing. Used to be a timber yard along there and all. Could've still bin there. Used to be nice blokes there, used to have some laughs. As I say, where I go, I don't care, really. It's up to you, really, if you don't make friends.

'School weren't too bad. Used to go that one down Park Avenue, East Ham. Had clubs at night time, you know, club nights. Like drinking and games and everything. Sometimes used to get in trouble – you know, had to stand outside the headmaster's room. Oh, didn't have to do anything, somebody tells the people something, and they come and get you, like. Put you outside the head's office. Just stand there! Don't know what I'd do now! No, used to be all right.

'Did different things. Used to play the old marble game, you know, cigarette game, you know the old flick cards and that. Used to have fights over it! Oh, fights everywhere! Then when me dad was here, I used to live round Boleyn Road, where the old Club used to be, Working Man's Club at East Ham. And one night, climbing, wasn't I, and a dish come down, cut all me lip. Cor, blood everything! I was climbing on like the sideboard. Not trees, didn't believe in climbing trees. Indoors. Used to play football outside. You know. Woman said, "don't play near my winders!"

'Used to be the old fire, the old toasting fork. Used to be lovely, yeah, used to be good. As I say, we used to sit on the wall outside and everything. Used to be friends next door, like. He used to say, "come over the gate," got a big Alsatian, climb over there and play darts with him.

'Wasn't too bad. I got two sisters, one brother. Don't see me brother much now, really. Sister I don't see, sometimes I do see the other sister, like. Lives in Barking. Dad? He used to do body work, lorries and that.'

And at the Friary? 'Oh, we've had some laughs, we have, yeah. As I say, I do some things – it might not be my job, but you know, I'd rather do something and day goes quicker. I've had some laughs. And as I say, me and Alan go out, I do removals, they say it's light removals, it's never really light removals, you know! We done one at Canning Town. Ought to see the state of the house! Really, you wanted overalls on, and gloves and that. He was right old, though – not nice to say, but I reckon he should be, like put away, in a home. Don't see many like that, no, not really. But he'd rather stay the way he is. But terrible, terrible he was.

How did he come here? 'I done an agency' – training – 'at Barking. And I had to come up here, and they asked me what I wanted to do, I said gardening, and had a little talk up here and that, and I got the boots, overalls and all that, and that's how Julian got me. We're all trades, I think! Don't think there's anything we haven't done here.'

Does he mind so much work without pay? 'No, not really, no. Well it's the old people, really. They can't, you know. You can't turn round and say "right, we don't do your garden, gotta give us money first." Can't do that. Done some really bad gardens, and all. We done one down Green Street, must've found about 50 balls where the kiddies bin throwing them over but they couldn't find em cos the garden's so bad, all the rubbish and that. But you see some of the gardens when we done them – I'm not being big-headed, but they're pretty good, you know, pretty good.'

Happiest times of his life? 'Nothing, really. Nothing important. See, I have to do me washing, cooking, do everything meself, really. When I get round to it! But you know. If I do something wrong, it takes me a while to get over it. You know. I lay in bed sometimes and think about it. It still seems the following day, like, I think what I've done, bad or whatever. But I usually go off anyway, after a while.'

West Ham? 'Yes. Always bin a supporter. Mum and Dad used to come from the market, used to see me standing right by the ground. But got all seats now, hasn't it, got all seats. Well, they reckon it's safer, you know what I mean, it's safer. But as I said, since they put the seats in, I haven't bin going. Too much money. Rather listen to it on the wireless! I played when I was at school, cricket and all. Didn't win, but we played! I used to enjoy me sport and everything, watch it on telly, or over the park.'

But getting a job – 'it's unbelievable, it is. Gotta have a CV and all that, you know. And driving! I say "I can't drive!" And if you do a cab thing, you got to have four-door car. But that's one job I wouldn't do, cab driving. It's in the night-time, you know? You get like two blokes in, or four blokes, what's the driver – what chance he got on his own?

'When I left the last job – no, wasn't that easy, you know. Wasn't that easy to get a job really. No. As I said, there is one still going, at Canning Town, but – stay here now. Cos if you start that one, if that shuts down you've got to come back here, and be lucky if you can, you know.

'No, I've had some nice jobs, enjoyed meself over the years. Nothing really to complain about, really. Ain't got nothing to complain about really. Done things that's gotta be done, and that's it. Yeah.

It all began during the summer holidays. I was suffering from a severe bout of boredom when one of the barmaids at my parents' pub suggested that my mother take me along to Anna Scher's Children's Theatre in Islington.

On arrival, I was disappointed to discover that there was a waiting list of a full year. So I added my name, and my mother and I decided that we would sit at the back and watch. After about half an hour, they asked me if I would like to join in. The lesson was about improvisation and oh boy, what fun I had! My ferocious tantrums were actually encouraged. I had never had it so good. After that evening, I was practically counting the days.

I had never enjoyed myself so much. It was an opportunity to use my imagination to the fullest and it wasn't very long before I was being asked to audition for television parts. But first I had to obtain my acting licence. My headmistress was approached for permission for me to have time off from school. After assurances that I would be provided with personal tutors, she gave in. My acting career was off and running.

I had quite a few parts for television companies, from an extra in an episode of *Pennies from Heaven* to one of Fagin's boys in *Oliver Twist*. But my biggest part was for BBC's Horizon, in which I played the younger brother of a disabled man called Joey Deacon. The programme was a big hit, won quite a few awards and ended up being shown all over the world.

When you were filming, you always had your own chaperone. Boy what fun I had! I gave them merry hell. "I want a drink, no, not orange, I want coca-cola. I want a sandwich, I want some crisps." Well, you had to make the most of it.

A lot of people don't realise how boring filming can be. Waiting for one of your scenes. Doing the scene over and over and over again until the director is happy. Only then will they actually go for a 'take'. Then it's back to making more unreasonable demands of your poor chaperone.

But I wouldn't have missed the experience for the world. It's probably one of the best outlets for energy that a child can have. Oh, and you got paid for your hard work. Yep, on the whole, it was pretty cool.

Jason

Doreen's story

Doreen is 62 and younger than her years, dark, well dressed and intelligent with a dry, self-deprecating humour. Her voice is expressive, acting out her moods – always with that touch of detachment, self-mockery. She assures me she's nothing of interest to tell. Just an ordinary life...

'I was born on 21st of September 1936 which makes me a very ancient lady of 62. I was born in Grant Street, around this area. Just an old terraced house.

'I made friends with a girl whose father owned the bakery, and I remember going in there with her, and coming out with one of these long buns with the icing on, which was absolute luxury to me. Prior to that, I can remember this horse and cart, and this man had a swing on the back that went round and round and round. And I remember standing in my cot and screaming and screaming and screaming to go on this thing. And I can't remember to this day whether I ever got on that ride. I think I did – to shut me up! And I remember this big picture of Christ, it was in my bedroom. He was just standing there, with his hands together, praying. And I remember my mother telling me that it belonged to her mother.'

When she was three, 'we were bombed out, I remember going to live with my grandma, in a very overcrowded house. We had one of those old Anderson air raid shelters, and I remember the damp smell, and this little oil lamp. Oh, I wanted to be up there watching, and I remember the searchlights going across the sky, and hearing the boom, and the guns. But it was so unreal, being a child, like a great big adventure, except when I was taken away from home. Didn't like that. I was evacuated with my brother Bill, crying my eyes out. Awful. And we went to Lancashire. I stayed with a very wealthy man, he used to look down his nose at me. Children shouldn't be seen. You know.

'My brother stayed on a miniature farm, and I used to spend every spare moment on the farm. We had guinea pigs, and chickens, and great big sunflowers. And I remember getting stung by a bee. Did I tell you about the coffee? Went to this house, and she said "would you like some coffee?" And I looked at her vacant, I'd never tasted coffee in my life. Didn't know what it was. It was awful, being away from home, didn't matter how nice people were to you. Just being home. With my mum and dad. We weren't a lovey-dovey family, but – it was just wanting to get *back*. I didn't understand what was happening. I didn't take it in about the war. All I knew is I was being taken away from my mum, the place that I loved.

'When we came home after the war, we ended up in West Ham Buildings. They sort of had a bathroom, but you used to have to hot up a great big enamel tin bath to get the hot water off the cooker. And then we were given a new council place. It was a lovely flat, a maisonette.

'Ashburton Road School is pretty rough. My mum sent me to school in what they used to call a gym slip, pleated thing, and the kids took the mickey out of me for wearing that. They used to go round in little gangs, it used to terrify me a bit, I just had a friend of my own.

'We weren't well off. Just an ordinary working class family. My dad – evidently he was at sea all the time, a seaman. This was before I was born. But my mum said she never saw much of my dad, and she was living

---

Sister Shooting Star

It was a cold November night
Voices! in head the head
my schizophrenic illness was
playing up afflicting me
I walked out to the quiet still snow
in the frosty night air spark
    sparkled all the myriad stars
Suddenly I saw her yellow and orange
streaking to earth spelling out my name.
Sister Shooting Star! And I knew my
young love of past years was thinking of
me two continents apart
across wide black space empyrean shooting
for whoever within sends me
Sister Shooting Star
and thus, well, soft poet-friend of mine
        it was.

John the Buddhist

on a pittance, you know. There's five of us. My mum kept the home spotless, over-spotless I would say. We always had plenty of clothes, plenty to eat, but there was no – what I can see in families and what I did with my own children – there was no cuddles. And my dad – I always called him Victorian. My mum used to stick up for me, because he was so strict, he really was.

'If a boy brought me home, didn't dare ask him in, in case my dad was there. I suppose he wanted his daughters – he wasn't gonna have them out street raking. And I remember my mum saying, "don't hang around with that girl, she's common, because she's got dyed hair, blonde" – it was her way of saying she's not a nice girl, you know, she smokes and she swears, which we never ever did. But he wasn't all bad, we used to sit and listen to some of the radio programmes together, Dad and myself.

'My mother always had to go out to work. She worked in Tate & Lyle's, emptying out the sugar bags. And she worked in a biscuit factory, Meredith & Drews. She used to bring boxes – you know you could buy the biscuits that were broken. When she was a girl, my gran used to take in washing, and my mother used to have to go round and sell bundles of firewood. She also had to go round where the coal used to be – they used to go and pick up all the old bits of coal. They were that poor. She was a cook in a big pub, Tidal Basin Tavern, it was called. She really worked very very hard all her life, my mum.'

At 15, Doreen 'sort of followed my sisters. They'd all worked for a big company called Lampson & Paragon, I was down the Custom House end. I remember saying to my mum that I wanted to stay on at school, because I wanted to be a dress designer. And my mum said, "girls don't stay on at school," she said "it's all right for boys, they can get a career, they've got families to bring up." But I was really really upset about that. I knew that I could have made a career. I wanted to be what I wanted to be – that was mine. But I wasn't allowed to go on to better things, so I chose shorthand typing. Well, I suppose it kept me in good stead.

'I remember earning 12/6d a week. My first wage packet. Course, I didn't use to smoke, or have any vices in those days! My mum took ten shillings, and two and six was mine. And I suppose that when I had the chance to get married, I took the chance, which I realised was a very foolish thing to do, because I ended up in another lot of aggravation. Nineteen, I was. My boy friend was doing his two years' national service.

'He's the girls' father, I mean we're divorced, but – we got married on one of his leaves. And then I didn't see him for nearly two years, he went to Germany. I stayed at his mother's house, and she was another disciplinarian. Oh, I tell you! My mother-in-law! There was the old-fashioned cooker, and the old-fashioned sink, and before I went to my office I had to do all the washing in the copper and leave that place immaculate, because I knew she'd go mad. I was working all the time, and my husband – we used to write to one another every single day. And then his sister got us half a house, upstairs flat. I was expecting my first child by then. Very lonely life. Then Susan was born.

'And then we had some really really hard times. He had a job as a driver's mate, and I thought look this is no good, we haven't any money. And the woman in the local shop said, "well you can clean my flat and the shop and I'll give you eight shillings." I had to scrub the shop out while there was people in and out, and I remember a woman coming in and saying "Doreen! What are you doing?" I felt humiliated – just didn't have the money coming in. And the woman downstairs she was – oh, another one! She used to bang on the ceiling – I only had Susan, and she was a quiet little soul.

'Then after Deborah was about three weeks old, we were going to move down to Melksham in Wiltshire, to stay with my cousin, see if we liked it there. They had a big garage in Bath, another one in Melksham, my rich relations! Audrey, she'd never known what it was to go without. I couldn't believe it! It was the other side of what I'd been used to. Going out for meals – all that sort of thing.

'My husband, Peter, was driving for the garage. And then we went to see this house that we were going to buy, just been built. And if only I'd have taken the chance. I was so frightened that we would have to pay a mortgage, and that's the biggest mistake of my life. I just did not dare. But he had a good job, it would have been all right.

'You wouldn't believe what sort of person I was. Absolutely naive. And I was very shy. The girls' father – he used to tell me all these things about life, and I didn't believe it. Especially about homosexuality. Was all taboo, you know. Even where babies came from. It was horrific, the way that I had to find out about life.

Doreen and Daphne at the desk

'Came back to London, we got another place. And I remember going up the Labour Exchange, and they said they need a typist in a solicitors', and I got the job there, and I stayed there for 30 years. I loved the work. My boss, he was of retiring age, nobody else would work with him. He was an absolute muddler. I more or less kept him in his job, I think. There was one boy, he was a petty criminal. But he was always up, and my boss used to buy the lad cigarettes just so that we could have his business. He was like a criminal himself, when you think about it. And then one day my boss called me in, this boy was there, and "he's got some dresses here for sale," what he'd knocked off! But oh, we did have some fun! There was lots of laughter. I don't know why I left. It was the silliest thing I ever did.

'I would have been very happily married for the rest of my life to the girls' father. But he told me about this, long after we were divorced, he said, "I remember I was about 46," he said, "and I panicked," like "oh! I'm gonna be too old, nobody's gonna like me." He must have had lots of little flings on the side. But this one, she was gonna tell me that they'd been having an affair, and he had to tell me himself. And that was terrible, it really was, it broke my heart. There's no way of putting it, because – I was happy. I went to work and did what thousands of millions of other women do, but – you have to live through an experience like that, because you get a feeling *here* – I had that pain for a long long time.

'But after that, I did the stupidest thing of all. I was on my own for five or six years. I married this other man. Then after we got married, he changed from that nice person into – oh – jealous. He was like Jekyll and Hyde. Anyway, I left him three times and went back – I was lonely, I suppose. And then I walked out with my mother's clean washing in a shopping trolley and my savings book. And I made my way round to my mum's and the best part of a year living with her, sleeping on the floor.

'And then I got the place I've got now, and I started getting my confidence back, and started to make the place look nice, and the garden. And then the best thing of all happened, I phoned the Friary up, because I wasn't working – my mum had been living with me for two years, and she got ill, and eventually passed away. And I remember walking in, Rose was on the desk – oh, she welcomed me really well. I sat in this armchair, and I couldn't quite make out who these people were that were shouting, laughing.

'And my daughters said, "you are like a new person, you've come alive." Just by being with everybody, and laughing with them. I said to them, I've got so many friends. Because I used to call myself the Lone Ranger. But I used to pray to God that I would find something to do in my life. I would pray and pray. And it seems I've had my prayers answered. Because he brought me here, and I just can't thank him enough.

'Yes, it's a wonderful place, here. There's love all around. I mean we get arguments. But it's like being in a big garden, I can see out there now, and Jesus saying, "suffer the little children to come unto me." Well, we aren't little children, by any long streak, but it's the same sort of thing, saying "you can come to me, and I'll help you if I can." Instead of saying "oh that one doesn't look right, speak right," doesn't matter what you are, you're accepted, till you can't be because you've done something really wrong. And though what I do is not a lot, you certainly get back more than what you give.

'I've had three good daughters. I've got five grandchildren, I'm very proud of them. When I had Susan, she was in a little cot, and I remember turning and looking up at the sky, and I thought I was the cleverest woman in the world, and the luckiest. I thought I had performed the miracle of all miracles.

'When I think about it, that was the time my mother really cared about me. When I went into hospital to have Susan, the actual birth was over, and she's told me that she'd phoned the hospital to see if there was any news, and the nurse said, "who's speaking?" And she said, "this is her mother." So she said "oh, I'll have to go and get Sister." And she said, "it frightened me, because I thought you had died. The relief when the Sister told me." So I realised that my mother loved us very much.

'But she didn't know how to show it. I suppose p'raps the way she was brought up. Because she was 13, and she had child in arms to look after, plus all her other brothers and sisters, while my gran was working in munitions. They called her the little mother cos she was looking after all the kids. And in those days it was all the old baths and rubbing board and mangle, and she had to do it all. So she didn't get an awful lot of schooling. You know, the day when she was waiting to be assessed whether they would take her into hospital, she turned to this care assistant and she said, "you know, I've got the most wonderful children." Because we did really look after our mum. I suppose it was because we had been so well looked after, you know?

'Oh, I loved it when my children were young. I always had a houseful. They just used to come in and I'd say "want a cuppa tea?" Opposite of my own childhood, it was. All the kids down the street used to come. And there was little Frankie and his sister Mandy, she always used to be holding him by the hand, little street urchins, they were. And we got a little tiny old caravan down at Blackwater. And I said to Frankie, "would you like to come with us to see the seaside?" He didn't even know what the seaside was. But I shall never forget him sitting along the seawall, his little face, he couldn't believe what he was seeing. And the caravan was always overflowing with kids. Oh dear, we had some times! The caravan would rock with laughter, it was such fun. And then we said that when our own children had grown up, we were gonna foster, but we never ever got round to that, because of – life. Life changed all that. But then again, it's the way life goes, what it deals out for you.

'I remember thinking I would like them to have what I didn't have, I didn't mean monetary things, just to be theirselves. And now I can see it, the way they bring their own children up. Debbie, her house is never empty. The kids come in off the street, and it sounds just like my house did, full of laughter, full of shouting, everything. Normal-day life, really.

'And now, as I say, it's lovely to be here. Soon as I walk in, sort of enfolds you and you're back amongst the family. I often think to myself, if I had nowhere to go, if something happened to me, I know I could go there, just till something better come along. If there is anything better.

'Prayer – I think prayer helps you. I mean, I always say my prayers at night. Always imagined myself, I don't know why, sitting on the beach, all alone and thinking, what do I want to ask for from God? And I used to say, "keep me well, and strong," then I used to think, I'm always asking. But I suppose in a way, God being here, in Helping Hands, you're paying back in some way or another. Must do, I suppose.'

It was May 1941 and that night would be full moon. We knew that it would be a bad night for air raids. During the day I had been out, testing new telephone lines not far from Central Telegraph Office near St Paul's. The bombs were always knocking out the lines somewhere.

The raid began early. The underground shut at once. A bomb fell near the Mansion House, so the buses could not get through. Glass was falling everywhere. I decided it would be safer to scramble through to the safety of the ten-storey building of the Central Telegraph Office. The incendiary bombs began to fall. When I reached the office, a bomb had hit the building and the top was on fire. Firebombs and bombs were falling everywhere. The building which St Paul's choristers lived in was blazing but they had been evacuated. It is now a beautiful garden.

The ground was covered with rubble and glass, hoses and water everywhere. I was herded into a corner by Paternoster Row by the air raid wardens. I told the warden I was from Central Telegraph Office, and he said "go to King Edward Building," which was the headquarters of the Royal Mail. The road was hot with the fires and debris falling. I was told they could not take in people from other buildings, but I had a pass which said in an emergency I could travel on any telephone vehicle or mail van. They said if I liked to risk it, I could go with the driver who was taking equipment needed at Stepney. There was not much choice.

The firemen had cleared a way, and we started out. We could hardly breathe. With difficulty, we got to Aldgate, but Petticoat Lane was ablaze and we could not get through. The driver forced a way through an alley. It was a residential area, with small shops. Still dangerous, but not so much danger of being buried under falling walls of warehouses. Out on the Roman Road, it was almost quiet after what we had left. We arrived at the telephone exchange. Then out to Stepney. What a relief. I spent that terrible night, one of the worst, in the cable chamber underground, which was used as an air raid shelter.

Next morning, devastation; but work was going on. The main roads were being cleared, debris and glass piled up. We got back to Central Telegraph Office. The engineers and army signals were getting temporary lines to Reuters and Cable & Wireless. Only the ground floor could be used. The many injured had gone to hospital, but they were bringing out the dead. Eighty-seven operators and teleprinter operators had been killed in this building alone. The King Edward Building was a shell, burned out during the night. Exhausted firemen still damping down fires were being served food, brought in from somewhere. There was no gas or electricity and only polluted water.

Eventually, I got back to Plaistow. My mother did not know if I was dead or alive. She was glad to greet her filthy-dirty, hungry daughter. She had spent the night with neighbours who had a Morrison shelter. We had to go and fetch water in a bucket from a standpipe in the street. Not much water for washing ourselves or our clothes.

We thanked God for our safety.

Susie

4 *The inhabitants*

Old John's story

Old John's voice is slow and strong; each word has its individual life, separate from the next. As if he values each word for itself. His hair, tied with an elastic band, is white; he often wears a bright silk scarf around his neck. He's 82.

I've bin more or less a workaholic, always on the go. Born in the same house more or less, only a few yards away, in Katharine Road, which was called I think White Posts Lane, years gone by. And around, where there's buildings, they were allotments, and the big house across the road where they used to ring the big bell for people who were working in the fields to come in for the meals.

My father was always on the go. His associates had a big furnishing store in Chelmsford. And somehow or other he came to London and married Mother, and they were in the greengrocery. But my mum and dad clashed. And that was the downfall of the whole fam'ly. They didn't divorce, but they both went their own ways, and may have bin a lack of money, because our house split into two flats, so there was five of us downstairs and I think seven upstairs. Fantastic, all what went on. And you had the old copper and that, outside toilet, hardly a patch of garden.

There's two sisters and myself. And they all left home, and my uncle had a radio and television, it was all radio in the olden days, and I would cycle over to my uncle and we would load the bike up with accumulators, and I used to take them round and put them on for people.

I don't think I did like school. I was scared. I became more or less top boy in the class, and I was glad to get away from home, so I was always at the gates before they opened. So much aggravation and anger, and I – I kind of hated my mother, because there was so much conflict. I tried to be clean, tidy, and I used to wear a button-hole. And I was one of the only boys had a watch and chain in school! When Dad was alive, I used to go round with him gardening and that. He was very ambitious man, but owing to conflict in the home, he couldn't make it. And he was a very clean man, and where others would wear a choker round the neck he would wear a smart collar and tie. Then Dad died early, I was about 18, and Mother clung to me more and more, she went partly mental. And me two sisters, they got married quick.

I was always working, and about the only boy that had a bicycle, built that up bit by it. And like we formed a gang and we all slowly got bicycles and tents and we used to cycle down to Canvey Island. You would hire a bicycle about fourpence old money per hour, and share it amongst yourselves. And we all put ha'pennies and pennies, we go in Woolworths and buy a tin kettle for sixpence, oddments like that. I was mainly interested in getting away from home as much as possible. I used to come home from school and be cycling all round Essex in the evening. And I could go all day without food and never thought about it.

I left school, 14, and the man next door was working in the Commercial Cable Company in Wormwood Street, and he said "would you like to be a messenger boy?" I'd never bin up in London, and seeing these vast buildings! Oh! it shook me a bit. We were a very americanised uniform people, we had lovely bow ties. And amongst all the messenger boys in London we were the highest paid, our wage was 14/6d.

Anyway, me being I suppose a go-getter, but a very quiet lad, I would comply with authority, so I became top boy. We had about eight lads, all from like East End. And from there, I went down Houndsditch in one of the big wholesale tools. That was another int'resting job. But see, times were hard, and anybody working on the buildings, they were lucky to get a job, and we used to get the various men, they would buy one pair of line pins for bricklaying and they wouldn't have the money, and they would go on the building site and be lining up outside of the shop in the morning, pay their money.

And there were a lot of horses, and you had the men running around with a little hand broom, keeping the roads clean. And men, they were standing there in the gutter with a basket with all maybe apples, chocolates, terrible, you just imagine today, used to literally stand in the road. But next door to us there was two or three young lads, they were German, I got on very well with them.

See, we had the Blackshirts and all that. Thing I didn't like selling was knuckledusters. We used to have iron ones, cost only 6d, or real brass ones, 2/6d. Couldn't do it, sell them. And somehow I thought war was coming on, because we were building various shelters, reinforced, under railways and that. I thought war, but I didn't read daily papers, I was too caught up in other things.

In the meantime, Dad was working down the docks. You were taken on daily. The gov'nor, he would stand up on the platform and you would crowd all round, and if he liked you, he would throw you a brass coin and that gave you permission to work. And after a time my dad died, and I took over his ticket. So I was the youngest dock worker. About 18 or 19. If you were taken on by the day you had to chase around to find a wheelbarrer which was usable, and you started unloading apples, whatever it was. You kind of got in the swing of work, and somehow I must've bin very fit, very wiry. I was a vegetarian, and I used to take about two slices of bread and a bit of cheese and that would last me except for little tin can of strong tea.

What kept me going, I think, what I call fighting authority. I saw management taking advantage of workers. Workers in those days didn't have two ha'pennies to a penny, and if they didn't do what the gov'nor said – out. And down the docks, you weren't allowed to go to a canteen for tea. No time for sitting down. Every morning, wouldn't know if you had work. There was a paper which gave you where the boats were coming in, so if you couldn't get a ticket one, you would chase to the other, trying to get a ticket, between quarter to eight and eight o'clock.

And when the war came on, I was the age, I think about 21, they called me up and I said no. In the meantime, I thought what's all this trouble, all to do with the Jews and that, and used to have various groups around East Ham, religious and political. Anyway, I joined the Christadelphians, and they were conscientious objectors, so that's how I landed at the Law Courts. See, when I was young, when I saw all these men come home from the war, land fit for heroes, I – I used to see them wandering the street, or knocking at doors, "paint your letter box and knocker for a penny." That's how the government treated ex-servicemen.

And I remember saying to all my gang of lads, you know, you'll never get me going to war. And it's rather strange, at the time, I said I'll be the last one that's married. Well, I'm still looking around today! All my friends married. Some got killed during the war years, but we all had a close relationship, knowing, you know, how we were brought up and how we shared things and that.

Anyway, I went on the land and I became a rebel there. I was against all authority, treating their fellow-beings and making them do this and do that. I used to cycle all the way right out to Ongar every day. And then again trouble – I thought they were exploiting us and that. And the Conchies were really put hard to it by various farmers. But once the workers got to know you, they more or less treated you as human beings.

Anyway, I got thrown off the land. And they wanted to make me ambulance driver, and I told them, "before the war you weren't interested in us, but now you want us to go out and kill people, you want to give us a job." This is me, bombastic, when I think back! Anyway, I wouldn't tear around, even when a bomb dropped. There always be some official in the car wanted to get there quick, and I used to say "well I'm in charge of the car." But some people – as I say, I was detested, being a Conchie.

I forget where I went from there. I was always doing something, and so much property was damaged, I become a carpenter, handiman and that. I started going into healing homes. I got some kind of gift, I could go round and various herbs in the field would vibrate to me, in a slight way, would vibrate for particular illness and that. It's uncanny, just a little dewdrop, what that can do. When I was on the land, to a degree I had some power to attune, only slightly, so various plants kind of vibrate to me.

After the war, I went down to a community that bin set up for Conchies. The one who had laid out all the money, buying the farm, she lived in East Ham. And she was being exploited. Anyway, between the two of us, we straightened the farming side out. She was a Buddhist in those day, but the farm, that went from the Buddhist way of living to fattening animals for market. You couldn't manage any other way.

Then I went my own way, various places. I suppose, looking for the God Within. See, I was never happy within myself, and the only way I got happiness was helping other people. And I saw so much cruelty done for money, that I wouldn't take money, I'd go and work anywhere that I thought was you know, adding to society. I would just work for my keep. We started a healing home for Mongol children. That was quite a big do. Then I went to other healing homes. I just keep moving around, various homes and that. I wasn't Christian, I don't think I really had any deep faith, it's mainly trying to help people, and as I say, when I was younger I put most of the world problems down to the Jewish, you know, wherever they went, they had all the money and causing all the trouble.

On and off I was doing decorating and painting and in between steel fixing. And I worked in Poplar hospital, I got paid there, I was a physiotherapist, so-called unqualified. And I was still living in East Ham and Dad had died, Mother was left alone and she clung to me. And my sister was so-called married during the war years, and the first kiddie died, and the next one survived, then the flat upstairs got empty and she moved in with so-called husband. And she found out he had a wife somewhere with about four kiddies.

In the meantime I got a job in the maternity hospital, and we were doing sometimes double shifts, and Mother wasn't well, and she wouldn't have anybody in. My sister couldn't cope really, so she wouldn't come, so it was left to me to try and keep things going, and being old fashioned house – and as I say, Mother died.

But I used to do quite a bit of voluntary work for the Quakers. They had various schemes going. Various parts of England, schools and that wanted paths laid. I did that on and off. I agreed with the Spirit within the person. But when I used to go to the Meetings, I found that I couldn't quieten my mind at all. And that took a long while to quieten the mind. Oh, it did with me, took years.

But you know, circumstances do affect you. I was a rebel because I didn't mind causing a rumpus, get kicked out, long as I change the conditions. Dad was Labour and that. I was very much int'rested in the Socialist Party but when I went into it, I thought all they were doing, they were condemning everything else and they hadn't lifted a hand and produced anything. And I was interested in people who were doing their best to make the environment better.

Old John, Garry and Donny

As I say, my salvation was helping people and living what I considered was a simple life. I used to go to all like the vegetarian movements and marches and that. Specially like Ban the Bomb, I went on quite a number of those.

I had various love affairs, but in a platonic way. I didn't know what love was. I didn't. Now, I respect women far more than I ever do the men. I think that's one of the reasons I decided not to marry, because men just abuse the women and have their own way. I watched me fellow man, and they all seemed to be working weekends, they wanted piece-work and I said I was against piece-work, so they wouldn't give me a job. I suppose poor rate of pay, men would hang the work out so they could work Sat'day and Sunday, I said if I'm married, I want to be at home, see the kiddies and see me wife over the weekend. I said all you seem to do, you work weekend and let your woman slave all Sat'day and Sunday, and you go to the pub, have your drink. I said what we want is a decent living, five days a week, so you can get home to your wife and children and enjoy them. See and if you've got the right partner, they keep you concentrated within certain areas. I'm at a tangent, I'm all over the place.

I'm a Virgo so I was criticising everything and everybody. That's why I have to be very careful today. But how I feel today, people are running after this and running after that, and they're not enjoying like the present moment. I was doing exactly the same. I mean I had such vitality, and I did a lot of fasting and got these psychic powers and that. But I used it for me own ego, and just by the grace of God I haven't vanished off the face of the earth. I mean the silly things I would do, deliberately abuse the body and that. I didn't know the first thing about loving the body.

But as I say, the older I get, I look around. Like you and I talking, amazing that there's vibration, there's a link! I mean, the wonder of the world, looking at the flower, the beauty, the sound, and having the faculties to see beauty and that in simple little things. I can't move along the street fast, I can look and see, all along the gutter, little plants growing. And eating the food, and appreciation of how it's grown – we don't give ourselves time to enjoy the moment. We want to fetch the next.

You know, I find I can't express what I think is an inner joy within me. I've had to learn the hard way. And I mean, there must be a reason why I'm still here. I got all more or less all faculties. I'm always looking over garden fences at the plants and kind of talking to them, and all the people rushing by, I know they have their own quiet times, but they don't seem to have time to stand and stare. I used to be the same myself. Well, I wasn't getting the inner joy in that. Yes, it was all ego, whatever I was doing.

I used to look at one particular magazine, and it had the advert for job across the road here. Must've bin about 12 years ago. It was 10 or 12 Brothers, and the chapel, I used to go in, and I didn't have a clue what they were doing. I did a certain amount of gardening. And then I had me allotment, and I had a lot of people local, I used to do their gardens or whatever. And I must've slowly settled down here. And then the night shelter started, about seven of them would come in every evening, and natter and make tea and really upset everybody, do their washing, have a bath. But slowly, changes – but Julian just went with it.

And I wonder now how much I've changed. I know there's a lot more within me got to open up. Especially regarding money. I thought that was the problem of the world and people killed for money, so what little money I got, I held on to, tight. It gave me independence, if I got thrown out a job, and I lived a very very simple life. And as I say, I used to do jobs for people, I'd say, "I don't want your money, you pass it on." I somehow wanted freedom. I partly think today, marriage – they seem to want to hold themselves together and not have friends, where I want to expand it, if I got a friend, I like to pass that friend on to somebody else. I think it's wonderful if you can do that. I remember reading a book, a lady, she said "I married the world."

In some way, I grieve because this wonderful world we've got yet people don't seem to find the time to appreciate it, or sit and talk. You know, I try and feel, even though I'm weeping, I enjoy this moment. Even though I've got other problems. But the moment is the moment. Little things, words, little shapes, I weep, because the mass of people are rushing by, say, and I say, "look at this little..."

It seems such a short journey I've bin on, and I think so many wonderful things, from all those dregs and all the unhappiness, there will be a glorious kingdom. And I s'pose through being hurt so much, I've always thought there must be a better way, and to a certain extent I feel I got some essence of that. But if you can, whatever you've got, hand it on, the enjoyment and that. All I'm trying to do, I'm trying to send out the beauty, the joy, the harmony I feel within myself. In little things and big things and that. I try and give it out to other people. I try not to condemn them, I try to look for the good where I never used to.

And that's why only last Sunday, waiting to cross the road, a fella, I could smell a bit of drink, and he started getting vicious, and then he kind of threatened me. I thought keep cool, you know, all of a sudden he gave in, but he could have bin nasty. I thought shall I cut up rough, I felt I could do it, but I thought, "bear

---

Apples

I was going to be the maggot in the apple, then – horrors – after a bite I could land in someone's stomach. The thought of travelling through the intestines and oh dear the exit into *what*? UGH! Or I could be tossed, inside my apple-travelling place, into a dustbin – no I can't bear that either – now I've crawled out of the apple and gone on my way. So that is the end of that story.

Apples – was it an apple with which the serpent tempted Eve? Who knows?

My husband adored apple pie. I wish I'd made it more often for him.

Apple trees with apples ripe and rosy. On a tree of gnarled bark. A home for birds. What fun to pick, and then the windfalls – food for foxes.

The apple has been part of our life and I guess the tree will go on growing longer than the length of our lives.

Brenda

up, John." See, when I get that capacity, I feel like – you know, go for them. But that's completely wrong! I'm creating more problems where I'm supposed to be a man of peace. Where I've got that power, I can do harm if I wanted, I think, "quieten down, John, be simple." And it's amazing how you can send out the peace, in various – it's not you, because your ego will never do it. You've got to call on the grace of God to use you – calm the situation down. I bin in – well, not like war, but my war's bin a different type of war.

Stop there, I think. Yeah.

Graham's story

Graham moves with a kind of deliberate slowness, bent slightly forward as if to gaze more closely at what lies ahead. His voice is cultured, not quite mannered – like that of an actor who has merged with his roles. Yet several times as we talk, he has to break off, go apart for a minute, be silent. He did his best, he told me, to keep sex out of it.

My family history is really pretty thin because what I know was related to me by my father, and men aren't very good at talking. I had a paternal grandfather who was famous as a drunk, and he used to keep the police at bay with his wooden leg. My dad was christened Zachariah Elijah Ellis. My mother, Rosa Edith Medlicott, comes from an old Cornish family.

I was born in London Hospital, and for the first three, four years lived in Knights Road, Silvertown. It was a nice little double-fronted Victorian house, in the shadow of John Knight's soap factory. I have this wonderful memory of waking up one morning and seeing a huge mound at the end of the garden that was all white. As the sun came up, it slowly went grey and then brown. And years later I asked my father what it was, and he said, "oh it was a pile of bones covered in maggots, they come out at night." Just after the war ended, I went back to Silvertown with my father and it was all flat, I couldn't believe it. And I can remember saying to my father, cos we had four bedroomed house in Barkingside, I said did people actually really live in places like this? I was about seven or eight at the time. The smell was still there. The most disgusting smell.

My father was a wonderful man. He was kind and gentle, he hit me only once, and I do see why. He had raked out the end of the garden absolutely beautifully, he did it every spring, and put in the seeds for the vegetable garden, and I discovered that my white rabbit had lain on her baby rabbits and most of them were dead. So seeing this wonderful patch of smooth earth, I made plots all over it for the baby rabbits and my father just hit me. And I bit his finger. And we retired.

Silvertown factories, and the old bridge over Bow Creek.

He brought me up on his own, he had a full-time job, John Knight's, had to walk miles when he was on shift work, cos there were no night buses then. He was just a wonderful, wonderful man. He taught me to read and write before I went to school. I adored him. But marrying my stepmother – when I left to go to college, that was it, the ties were cut. He was born in 1884, he was 52 when I was born. My eldest brother Frank used to torture me. He liked giving me Chinese wrist burn till the skin split, and tickling me till I cried, then calling me a cry-baby, great fun. But my brother Peter, although he was rarely around, he's always been my friend and supporter. I love him dearly. I used to go and see him before I left home, once a week, just to get away. He was running a place in Covent Garden market, I used to go and work there in the summer. He left his first wife and disappeared. Strangest thing. I was walking down a road in London, years had passed, and there he was, driving this smashing little red male menopause sports car.

My mother died when I was six, and I was sent away to the country where

I was raped by an older boy. Which seemed, looking back, to set a pattern for sexual abuse which lasted till I was about 10. Dad married when I was about 11. It was a disaster. Poor lady didn't really have a chance. I escaped when I was 16 and went to art school, where I met my first lover, Eric Hebborn, and we lived together until I was 32. I didn't think of doing anything else but drawing. I kept for years in my mother's bible a piece of stiff lavatory paper that I had drawn on, two little mice. They were rather nice. I'd always known I was gay. There was never any inner struggle. I was lucky that it just seemed the most natural thing in the world. It is the most natural thing in the world for me.

So Eric and I went to live in the most wonderful house called the Cumberland Hotel, a series of late Victorian houses in Highbury. Eric was at the Royal Academy Schools, winning prizes, but in the main we lived off my grant. Our first summer holiday was a sheer idyll. We lived in a tent on the edge of the marshes in Maldon, covered by huge old willows. It was probably one of the happiest times of my life.

The Cumberland was run by a very strange man called Mr Davis. He didn't want anyone to know he owned the place, he was just "the manager", and he lived under the stairs in this tiny cubby-hole. He showed us one day a steel-doored room, basement room I suppose about eight feet by ten, carpeted to about six, seven inches, in pound notes, £5 notes, £20 notes, £50 notes, that obviously he couldn't take to the bank because the tax people would be on him. It was wonderful.

And not long after we'd been there, we ran out of money and broke open the gas metre. Next morning Mr Davis came in to empty the gas metres and said, "hello gentlemen, what's this," and we were still in bed. And he said, "oh I'd never have thought you would have done that, I always reckoned on you as two gentlemen sharing." He was a wonderfully excitable man, a true Dickensian. So Eric picked up this little painting he had been doing, signed it "Sickert", with paint and quick-drying varnish, waved it about a bit, then said, "well, you can have this painting and sell it, that will cover whatever we've taken." So Mr Davis looked at it and said, "I don't call this a painting," he said, "you are joking already?" he said. But he sold it for £100, which in the late '50s was a lot of money. He was jubilant.

Mr Davis started up a club called the Lucifer Club. There would be the most terrible fights. Then a couple of "Gentlemen" turned up and said they would see there were no fights if Mr Davis would keep it open. They were a north London gang. We had no idea that they really were criminals in the sense that they did really horrible things. I was really pissed off with Eric, because he kept sneaking around sleeping with boys, and pretending he hadn't. And there was a lovely boy called Dougie. He invited me out, and it was great. Eventually Dougie and I had sex. It's a nice story, because it was the first time Dougie had had sex with a man, but he'd always wanted to, so that was fun, and one up for me, I was beginning to feel a little rebellious. And one night somebody said, "you wanna watch yourself with Dougie, he carries a razor." So I said, "why does he carry a razor?" "Well," he said, "he goes round and collects money, and if they don't pay he cuts them." So when Dougie came round, I told him. He said, "oh, Gray, don't worry, I'm not gonna cut you!" And I thought well, I didn't actually think you were, Dougie, I just didn't want to get in the middle.

Eric went to Rome. I got into the Royal College of Art and won a scholarship to Italy, went down to see him, terribly upset to find he had a pretty little Sicilian boy. So when Eric came back, he had been living the Dolce Vita life. I was still at the Royal College, still living at the Cumberland Hotel. – This is mainly, at the moment, about Eric, because I was trying to be a dutiful wife, you know? – None of the galleries were interested in his work. Mine? There you go. I was doing some drawings for an Oxford magazine, and Eric went totally beserk. I used to draw on the floor, and he kicked over the ink and water and stamped on the drawings. So I thought, well, there's one painter in the house, which happens with most women who live with painters. And I was in love, and it didn't seem a sacrifice, he was just a brilliant draughtsman and I believed in him.

So he took up forgery. And we bought a lot of stuff from a wonderful woman called Marie Gray, a gorgeous Edwardian woman. We started up a little gallery called Panini Gallieries. Didn't sell a thing, except Eric's forgeries. So we moved to Rome.

We lived in this wonderful villa, up in the mountains above Tivoli. Leontine Price used to come and stay in the villa opposite. I remember one spring morning, the village band came down to play, which they did every Easter, and it was the most awful noise. I went to get a thing of wine, and bread and cheese and money, and as I was getting things together, I noticed this incredible figure in this huge Hawaian dress, big straw hat, come floating down clapping her hands, started to conduct them. Into the Easter hymn from *Cavaliera Rusticana*. Which she started singing. And it was so incredibly beautiful. The mountains made a kind of curve so you could hear shepherds and people working in the vineyards, like a Breughel picture, people working up there on the hillside. It made a natural amphitheatre. She had a glorious voice.

Eric became very successful, forging. He kept sleeping around, I wasn't working, and eventually I left. He had taken all the money from our joint bank account, so I left at 32 without any money, without any idea what to do, no training, because I'd spent the time – I'd chosen it – being Eric's studio assistant, housekeeper, wife. It's not woeful, I don't think it was wasted. It was difficult to leave, because I loved Eric. But I wasn't allowed a life of my own. And I think 32 was a good time, it wasn't too late for me.

I stayed in Rome for about eight months, got a job, got myself a little 16 year-old boy-toy, very sweet boy, actually. Then came back to London. And had no idea what to do.

There's a wonderful club behind Oxford Circus called the SpeakEasy. I used to go there. And one evening I got a shirt and I painted it in kind of zebra stripes in black and brown, very carefully, and wore it down there. And this guy came up to me and said, "where did you get that shirt?" He offered me the most ridiculous – something like £50, and shirts then at the most cost £10. And it still didn't click. Not for a few further months. And I said gosh, I could make money. So a ghastly woman had this little boutique, she and her partner. And they discovered a warehouseful of the most wonderful chenille velveteen curtains, which they made dresses out of. So I started handpainting for her, got myself a gorgeous little studio. Had a medieval cellar, and I used to go down to

Piccadilly Circus and pick up the boys and take them back. Because this woman had carpeted it and put mirrors in all the archways, so it was a gorgeous garçonniere. Worked incredibly hard, which I adored, started painting fabric for several designers. Really great. Then I started dress designing. And was really having the best kind of bachelor life. Earning a lot of money, living very well, having a lot of sex.

And then I met John. John Kenneth Elliker. I used to take a bus or tube somewhere I'd never been to, and work my way back into London, drinking bitter. And when the pubs closed, go clubbing. Then if I hadn't scored, I used to go out to the local cruising place. And one night I went out to the Putney towpath, and there was little John standing there. Yes. There's an old music hall song, it goes "when you fancy you're past love" – so trite, but it's so true – "when you fancy you're past love, it is then that you meet your last love, and you love them like you've never loved before." So I moved in with him in Putney.

We both had a lot of baggage. He had been sent to approved school and borstal and stuff, and then abused, and I suppose my abused stuff. We had the most terrible rows, which neither of us could understand. We used to go to this marvellous pub, tiny, narrow little pub, and at the further end were all the hippies, then in the middle were the minor criminals, and at the top were the police, then round by the fireplace were actors and writers and the hardened criminals. And somebody once said to me, they said, "God, if I could just once have somebody look at me like John looks at you, I'd be happy." I just took it for granted. You know? One takes so much for granted. And it's really sad, and really strange, how we seem to learn only by trauma. We don't seem to learn very much by laughter. Any rate. We used to have the most terrible rows. And the most wonderful togethers. He is the love of my life. My love partner.

I was designing fabrics like mad, and I got a bit pissed off. I went on a holiday to California, and loved it so much, it was so clean, this was in 1978, England was looking particularly grungey. And I decided California was a good place to be. So we had a pretty little apartment, and John started up a business, apartment maintenance, housepainting etc.. And I thought fuck, I don't want to be stuck in all day, I'll work with John, so that's what we did for several years. I loved it. Then I got a job at this totally eccentric publishing house, mainly children's books, very lovely picture books actually. We had this lovely old mission-style house on the edge of a canyon, with kestrels nesting in the eave and skunks coming round. Skunks are so tiny. And they think, like mocking birds, that they're totally invulnerable.

Eventually John got this wonderful job, in charge of a property company's holdings, which meant he had to drive all all over San Diego county, up into the mountains, down to the sea, just checking on properties, writing them up, having lunch. And at weekends I used to go with him. He got a wonderful apartment, California dream apartment.

And then he became ill. And died. I think really that's all I want to say about that.

I didn't know what to do. I tried to kill myself with John, but it didn't work. So I started up a children's publishing company, called Medlicott Press, and that was incredibly successful for a few years. Partly through luck, I got Simon Schuster as distributors, which was great. Then they were taken over by Paramount Studios, sales began to go down. Then Viacom bought Paramount Simon Schuster and about 200 small companies which they wiped out immediately. Capitalism at its best. And I managed to get through to somebody, enquiring about my books, and she said, "oh they've been trashed." I spent a lot of money, thinking I would sue.

My brother Peter had come out to stay with me often. And one time, he brought this huge bottle of Hennessy VSPO champagne brandy, glorious, and we sat drinking it, and he said to me, he said, "I don't approve of your life style, I don't approve of you being gay," he said, "but I want you to know that whatever you do, I love you and I always have." And that meant a great deal for me. For a moment I did think of standing up and saying, "what do you mean you don't approve of my lifestyle, who gives a shit?" But it was a big step for him, he's your typical middle middle class, *Daily Mail Daily Telegraph* conservative. Big step.

Channel 4 were doing a programme about Eric, who I believe was murdered by the Italian art mafia. He had just written a book on forgery which upset them very much. At the same time my brother had a heart attack, so I came to England, started working on a proposal for a programme about Eric, and realised there wasn't any point in going back. Also realised that I was just about penniless. And so I ended up here.

I remember saying to Julian that in a sense I was glad my company had gone bankrupt, because I was settling into the kind of life that I was leading before I met John, which was okay when you're 30-something, but I don't think it's okay for me – for somebody – in their 60s. I wasn't evolving. I was sort of treading water.

I remember saying so many times, I'd like to be a good person. I was always told to be a good boy, you know, "be a good boy because Mummy's not here, you've got to be a good boy for Daddy." I've turned myself inside out to be a good boy. And one of the wonderful things about getting older is one makes time for reflection. You spend more time being still and you can do that by watching television, reading or you can get down to the essential. It's good when one has let go, not only of material possessions, that's silly, but all the other things. I'm not into this self-beating thing. It's like cigarettes. I know cigarettes will kill me, but I enjoy them and I would not enjoy giving them up. All the peculiar little vanities that every one of us has. Nothing ever goes – but I think what is meant by letting go is being aware of them. Being able, when one's in the middle of a little piece of nonsense, to be able to say haha! I know what this game is. And when you do strip all that away, you're left with a core. I'm not sure that my core is particularly nice, I'm not sure that I really would, if I'd had a choice, have explored it. But I'm just glad that through all the rebirthing, all the alternative therapies, John dying, I've at least come to the stage where I can see myself and accept myself. And even laugh at myself. It's wonderful being able to laugh at myself.

People here? Oh, they're family. I always felt totally outside our family. I mean I was always comfortable with Peter. He made me comfortable. But I never had a family till I came here. And I find it marvellous that everyone accepts me, because I'm very out, always have been. It's wonderful to be accepted by them, supported by them, at such a late stage in my life, it's an experience I've never had before.

When we used to go up Town, my father and I, 25 bus, he used to point out the window of the room where I was born. And so I felt a great sense of "that's where I was born." I remember the front of the house in Knights Road, had a little garden. But I was taken away from it so young that I don't feel a part – you know? it's so strange. I don't feel I'm not an East Ender, yet I don't feel I am an East Ender.

I went down with my brother to look at Knights Road. It doesn't exist any more. It's still on the map, but it's all banks of flowers and storage yards now, very strange. My father would have turned in his grave to realise such a thing was possible, that the docks are marinas. And it doesn't smell! It doesn't smell.

After my house was bombed 12 families from Plaistow were sent to Walsgrove, Colonel Buxton's home in High Beach. It was like a mansion. My mother and I had a four-poster bed. The house had no heating. It was freezing.

I had to come to Plaistow every day to do my work, and it was a long way to the station. Downhill going, uphill going back. I had to pass the church on the way. Often it was dark and rather eerie. There was a white owl in the churchyard, and somehow I felt as if I was home when he screeched as I went by.

The lady who was housekeeper to the Buxtons was later my mother-in-law. Her son came to Walsgrove on leave from Holland, where he was in the Artillery. We fell in love and I was proposed to in a field of daffodils in Walsgrove grounds. Could not get married for nearly two years, as Arthur was serving in the army of occupation. It must have been meant that we should meet in that way.

I went to the church in the forest. I helped make the carpet that is still in the church and some kneelers. My mother in law is buried in the churchyard and I often go there in the summer.

Susie

5 *The neighbours*

Doris' story

Doris lives in a maisonette on Balaam Street, just across the road from the Friary. Born in 1922, she walks now with difficulty and can go out little. She tells the story with a kind of matter-of-fact detachment, often with humour: these things happened, but it's the present that's more important – particularly her family, her grandchildren.

I was born at Canning Town, the house where we lived my mother was born there and all, and we lived there till, oh, 1948, I think it was. Dad died when I was eight years old, had my grandad living with us. And my sister, there was only the two of us, my sister and I. It wasn't too bad. I mean, weren't rich or anything, my dad used to work at Tate & Lyle's, and he died in 1930. And as we've got older, my sister and I have always said we really miss him more now than what we did when we was children.

Our house was in Shirley Street. No garden – yard, we had. My grandad used to go out every Monday morning, to light the copper to do the washing. Saturdays he used to say, "you want the copper alight, to have a bath?" He died in 1941.

Oh yes, they were good days. Church was just round the corner to us, St Luke's church. We used to go to Sunday school, they used to have a Play Guild one night a week. And one night a week they used to have picture shows, if you went to church on Sunday, you got your star card marked, if you got one star, you could get into the pictures. Then when you got to 14, 15, they used to have youth club. And every Saturday they used to have a dance. I think it was only records, but still it was a dance.

We'd do what we was told. Couldn't get away with much with my mum. Though I used to get away with more than what my sister did. And I stuck with my mum – when we moved out of Shirley Street, I went with her, then she lived with me here right till she died. Me and her had our ups and downs, you can't live in peace all the time, can you? But I mean, you've got your different age groups, you've got to give and take. Me and my sister say, "if mum was alive now" – I mean, my grandson gone and living with his girlfriend – oh! it would be murders! You can't do nothing about it these days, that's the way of the world, isn't it? In those days, you used to try and work it out. I suppose when I think of it, me and my husband could've separated, but we just sorted things out, and that was it. I don't think any of us ever thought of leaving each other, you know.

Used to have to find things out for yourself. I remember my mum saying, when she was about 15, 16, she said her mother was talking to somebody, something about my mum's sister being pregnant, and then she realised my mum was standing there, and she said "get indoors you." She was about 16! I think the children now, they learn too much too young. They talk about it in school and they want to go and try it, don't they!

I was about 17, 18 when the war started. When the blitz started, got a bit bad, we went down to my uncle's place at Rayleigh, but we was only away about three weeks. We used to sleep underneath the arches, the viaduct, goes down to Silvertown. My sister and I were working in the City, both our firms got bombed out, 1940, the Christmas where all the City first got hit.

Anyway, my sister got married just after the war finished, 1945. She was still living with mum, and they both lived there. And then she got pregnant, and then when her boy was six months old she got a place, she was in a Nissen hut, and then our place got condemned. We moved down Hermit Road way, and we was down there about – oh, seven years.

In the meantime I'd met my husband. I'd been out one night, come home, have a nice bath, you know, got all me hair put up in curlers! Knock at the door, and it was my friend. So she said, "oh I'm over the pub," she said, "with George. He's got his mate with him," she said, "come over and keep me company." So she talked me round, I put a scarf on, I went over there, and that's who it was, fellow I married in the finish. And Dave was born, and just before that, he got put on another boat and it was going out to Korea. He was in the Navy. So he didn't see David for two years.

After the war, St Luke's, they used to run a youth club, and I used to go round there one night a week to help in the canteen. It was after I had my David and all, while Les was out in Korea. Actually, he was on the Belfast, you know the Belfast that's up London? He joined up when he was 16, that was in '37, yes, 1937. Then he got sent out – he was fighting in the Spanish Civil War. I didn't know him then, he was all over the place. But I mean while he was in the Navy, he was only home for a couple of weeks every so often. The only place he regretted not going to was Australia, he said he never got to Australia.

When he came out, he went down to Beckton gas works. He was doing a lot of overtime, but once the summer came he was on the flat rate. So he went down to Silvertown, and he worked there for nearly 30 years. Don't get people staying in job like that these days, do you? My brother-in-law, he was on the buses for about 30 years, 32 years, I think. Oh yes, he loved it.

When our place was condemned, we got put in a Nissen hut. Just corrugated iron. There were two bedrooms at the back, there was like your living room, and there was a little partition and there was your cooker and sink and worktop. That was like three rooms, really. Toilet was outside. Heat water, or else we used to come down to the baths, here on Balaam Street. About seven years we lived there, I was married from there. My mum and Les, we lived there, then David was born there, and Martin was born there.

Anyway, they started pulling these Nissen huts down, and they moved us round here. And I've been here ever since. That was 1954, December. I think it was in the January they opened the church. And course the boys started going to church, Sunday school and that. And they was in the Scouts, Brownies, the Guides, the Cubs. And they talked my husband into taking them, so he was the Scoutmaster. You'd get all the Brothers round there, the youth clubs, you know, and if they got a bit browned off, used to come over here, knew they'd get a cup of tea. And then in the evening, they'd all used to come over – I've had about six of them of them in here, all at once! I don't know if the older ones knew. I used to do their habits and all, make their habits!

But the Friary – one time a woman couldn't get through that door. I think we had a meeting one time, they let us go out the garden, I think it was when the Sisters were over there. Though they weren't at first, they was living in a house up the road here. They used to do a Christmas play round there – kids was always in it, so was Les.

We had plenty of cinemas round here, and we used to go up the West End and see different shows. But as I say, the area has changed a lot. I know I shouldn't say it really, but I think when all these immigrants have come over, that's altered the place a lot. Where I lived down at Canning Town, it was a dock area and we used to have a lot of coloured people come. I went to school with coloured people, so I mean, I wasn't racist. But I know I shouldn't say it, but I think I am now! I mean East Ham used to be a nice place, and Upton Park, but – oh, it's really come down. I don't know, it's just not the same round here now. I wouldn't go out on me own at night now. Don't say anything would happen to me, but that is just how you feel.

Neighbours? I speak to them, but I'm not one to be always in and out of people's places. People live next door, we was good friends, me and his wife, but she died, she's been dead about ten years. Me and her husband always speak when we meet, but most of that block are all new people now. See, as people have bin moving out, coloureds have bin moving in. I mean there was none in there couple of years ago.

Oh, I liked it round here. When I came here, this was like different class area, I would never've liked to have gone back to Canning Town. There was still a lot of the old neighbours there, but – I don't know, once you move from that area, it was different.

I mean, when I started work, you couldn't go up to Aldgate by train without going to Plaistow. And buses – they was a good service, but they used to be so packed. When you used to finish work, you used to have to fight to get on a bus, well, it was trams then, then they had trolley buses. During the war and all, traffic, oh, it was horrible. Because the docks was working full then, but now there's nothing goes in the docks, is there? When the docks went, a lot of people was out of work. And the factories down at Silvertown, there is still some factories, but not like it used to be. I mean, this was a proper dock area. I mean, I'm 77 now, and I've seen some changes.

There were lots of black kids. We used to play together, no animosity between any of us. There was white women married black, you know, West Indians,

The arches – Silvertown viaduct

they were working on the boats. Got on ever so well together. Played in the street, great big skipping rope right across the road. And we had a factory down the street so we used to have quite a bit of traffic, just drop the rope and let the lorry go over it. Everybody in the street used to speak to each other, and all the children used to play together. Sometimes when me and my sister's talking, we say "I wonder what happened to so and so," you know. During the war a lot of them went.

My mum didn't go out to work after she married, not after she married, she didn't. Her trade was dressmaking, she was apprenticed at it, and tailoring. And she was working down Tate & Lyle's during the war, first world war, that's where she met my dad. Was only married about 10 years, when he died. My mum taught me most of what I knew. Well, in them days they didn't do apprenticeships like my mum did.

Oh, you didn't have a lot of money. I mean, when I started work, was what – '36. Was doing underwear then, only earning 10 shillings a week. And that was right up the City, Moorgate. We used to take two shilling rise every six months. And by time I got bombed out there, I was still only earning 25 shillings a week. That's what everybody got. That was it. And course, went and found another job, and they offered me two pound a week. I thought I was well off! But you used to save out of that and all. Give Mum some money, she used to give you pocket money, whatever it was, and you still used to save.

When I started work, I was doing ladies' underwear, was all high class stuff. Used to send it out to Austria and Vienna, to have it embroidered, came back and then we made the things up. A pair of knickers – cheapest was about 12 shillings. More than what I was earning! One pair of knickers! They were Austrians, man and his wife, always spoke German to each other. And then when Hitler started invading out there, she'd got a sister out there, and she came over and she was working with us and all. Course they weren't German, they were Austrian. And then the man and his wife got interned, and she carried on the business. She was a refugee, she weren't interned.

I done uniforms during the war. Big place, side of Aldgate station. They done all uniforms there, I was on naval uniforms. Big change from underwear! I was there when the war finished, then me and another girl, we went into dressmaking. We couldn't get settled down, we was going from one place to another, half a day here and a day there! We could find the work, but we didn't like it. My mum never knew! As long as we'd got her money, we was all right.

And then we got a job, and we liked it so we stayed there. That's when I first went into dressmaking. Was all cut out for you, and they had someone else doing the finishing, hooks and eyes, things like that. We all got bundle of work, and we got to do that bundle. I was never – they used to call them conveyor belts – I was never on a conveyor belt. Always done a thing right out. When I worked on the uniforms, we done the tops and the other end of the room done the trousers. They used to work on a conveyor belt. Got this great big long row of machines, and do a certain part, and they was doing that part all the time. One girl would do pockets and another put bands on – I couldn't have done that. Then when the war finished, we started doing demob suits. They were horrible. We wasn't earning nothing, so we went! That was when we went dressmaking.

I worked after I'd married till I had David, then I didn't work no more, cos Mum was alive then. Mum died in '66. I didn't go out till about '67, and then I got job at Forest Gate, and I was there for 13 years. Place I worked, we had all great big long room. There was one, two, about five benches with machines, I think there was about a dozen on each bench. Do dresses, skirts, trouser suits, for the shops. That was the only time I ever done piecework. Just used to do ordinary timework, you know, do what you could. I didn't really like piecework, you had to rush it too much. I got made redundant from there. And I used to do it at home, so I was nearly always on the machine. I loved it, loved it. About '91 I think, I broke me wrist, and I've not done much since then. I was nearly 70 when I packed it up. Well, I think now, you've done your share, you know. But I used to love making wedding dresses. I made a lot, some beautiful ones and all.

My mum made my wedding dress. When my sister got married, rationing was still on, but luckily at Upton Park, there was a lot of Jewish shops down there, and if you knew the right one, you could get your things without coupons. You used to go down there, you daren't stop, cos they used to have somebody standing outside, "come inside and have a look" – they used to drag you in and you used to have to buy something, and you was just having, you know, nose round!

Stop being involved at the Friary? To be truthful, after my husband died. Always used to go to the church Sunday morning, but after he died I just couldn't go. Don't think I've been since. Oh, I was pretty involved round there, you know, on the parents' committee, and the Cubs and Scouts, and lady who was caretaker round there, Jenny – she's in the home down Chargeable Lane now, I think – she was the caretaker. In the finish she asked Les and I if we'd take a turn and clear the halls on a weekend, got too much for her, you know. And then when her husband died, Les and I took it on, we used to do it every fourth time till Les went in hospital. Been 15 years now. Yes. 1983, he died. We was married for 35 years, it would have been our Golden Wedding anniversary this year. Yes, would have been our Golden Wedding anniversary this year.

The eldest son, he's 49 this year, the other one's 46. And the girl's 43. All got two children each. Oh, I like going down to see them. The eldest boy's, they love me down there. "You haven't got to go home, have you, Nannie, why don't you come down and live here?" Lovely boy, Garry, he's getting married this year. I had him living with me for a year, he was here just over a year, 15, 16 months, then they're buying a place between them. Down at Purfleet, he is. So he's the nearest one to me, really. We got worried when he first left school, in case he got into trouble and that, but touch wood he never has.

David was in the grammar school, done all his GCEs. He stayed at school till he was 19, and in the end he went into Customs and Excise. And the other one, he went into banking. He just went to a comprehensive school, but he's done just as well, out of not going to a grammar school. And Lynne went to the grammar school, she went into civil service. And they've all done well for themselves, you know, considering the area they've come from. But as I say, we've seen a lot of changes round here.

They say to me, "Mum, why don't you move out of here?" But of course my sister, she don't get out, she walks around on two sticks indoors, she's got a wheelchair. I said no, not while she's here. I mean if anything was to happen to her, I'd be off like a shot! I would, yes. Really, she's the only thing I've got that keeps me here. Never lived no further than what we are now, apart.

She's got three granddaughters and two grandsons. My mum only had us two girls. We've always got on well together. I don't say we've never argued, but never fallen out good and proper, you know. I did with her husband, I didn't get on with him much. Till just before he died he mellowed, and I think I took pity on him then! He was a bit of a pig to her sometimes, you know, that's what got me down, and all.

Happiest times? I think the years just before I got married, you know, late teens. I behaved meself, I wasn't a naughty girl! The girl next door, they were people for having parties, and her dad used to organise a coach outing, day out to seaside, things like that, and we was always included. As I say, I used to go to St Luke's church, and every summer they used to have coach outing. Oh, we've had some laughs! Used to take the kids, used to have a lovely time. Stop at coffee place in the morning, then coming home used to stop at pub. Just half hour, something like that.

Don't need a lot of money, course you don't. No, don't need a lot of money.

Oliver's story

Oliver and Teresa Olivagi live on the second – top – floor of a block of 1950s council flats, with their son Solomon and Teresa's half-Ghanaian son Christopher. They are alike in being cut off from family and home community – and from the oceans by which they grew up. Oliver, small but strongly-built, is a Solomon Islander. His voice is very soft, warm, nearly always filled with laughter, at himself and the incongruities of life. His gentleness and apparent hesitancy mask a fixed determination once he knows what he has to do.

My name is Oliver Olivagi. My mother is called Janet, and my dad is Mason. I have three sisters, first one is Solomei, and the second Emily, and Dorothy. We all went to school. Solomei only went up to Standard 4. You know, probably about ten people from the whole island continue on and the rest, they just go back home.

Me and Emily managed to get a place in the senior primary school. We had to go away from the island, overseas really, it was kind of scarey. She went further away than me, 200 miles or something, and I went to the next island, Santa Cruz, which is only about four hours on a boat. I must have been about 12 then. It was kind of rough – it was the cyclone month, and the waves and the wind! They asked us to jump overboard and swim ashore! It was kind of exciting as well as frightening. I was used to swimming. Back home you don't have showers or things like that, every day you go down to the sea and swim.

Anyway, I got there. And next thing, we had to go to the hills to cut sticks, to make our own beds. I'm used to making bed, because in my other primary school, was boarding school, so I had to make my own bed. And in the afternoon we were given hoes, to go and work in the farm on the hill. And we did that every day, because we were more or less self-sufficient. We get some things like flour, sugar and rice, you know, I think the ship comes in every three months. But the other things we have to grow ourselves.

The second day I started to be homesick. The teacher who was taking us for reading was one of my aunts from my village. And when I saw her, that was it, I was crying like hell. Somehow I felt like I'm not alone, I've got my aunt here. Everyone from the island, we were like related – is a little island, everyone knows everyone else. I knew my parents could not afford for me to go home, so for three years I stayed in school. Didn't see my parents. I used to grow some potatoes, sugar cane, stuff like that, in preparation for the holidays, so I will survive! I think my school life was very happy. I tried to be good. Because we had this great thing of punishment, we had the cane or we would spend an hour doing manual work.

I was very ill once, and nearly died. But I think one thing that kind of comforted me was that I had my bible. I had it under my pillow. But there was an evangelist came to train students, he was really powerful. There was a healing service one evening, and I went to it. A few days before, I was building up, I was spending time in prayer. I was absolutely sure that I would be healed. There was singing, praying, and I went up to him, and he prayed over me and touched my back, and I just felt freedom, you know. I was healed, I felt it, from that moment on, I feel no more pain.

After school, I wanted to go with my friends. I was maybe 14. One of my uncles was then headmaster, he said "no, I'll send you home, you've been away for three years. Then you can go and see your friends." I think I went for six months home, I had to work to dry coconuts to make money for ship, to go to other island. I went with my adopted sister and her husband. And I stayed there for – two years? I was helping with the church work, sometimes I'd take the services in the village. And the people gave me some land, said "that's your land." This place was very exciting – the land that was given to my sister and brother-in-law was quite long way – if you go early in the morning, and is dry sea, see hundreds of crocodiles lying on the mud, you know, warming themselves up. Sharks, huge sharks, and turtles, and is kind of nice, you've got food everywhere! We catch turtles for feast, and crocodiles, used to catch them sometimes. And sometimes sharks, nice meat, but too strong.

And I think the councillor came back from a meeting in Santa Cruz, and he said there's going to be a secondary school! In same place where I went to school before. There were five other boys, we were accepted, so we went back to school. And there were only about ten people at the beginning of the first term. There was no dormitories, all the buildings were left, you know, to rot. So our main thing to do was to build dormitories and classrooms, repair all buildings. So it took us, I think four or five months, maybe. And also planting, potatoes and vegetables. And we were paid, and that was towards our school fees. And I had to dry coconut, sell it to the cooperative society and get money for my school fees. I hadn't seen my parents then for two years already.

This school, it's like a community training centre, where you are training people, whether business, woodwork, bit of mechanic, to repair like outboard motors, things like that. Not allowed to learn maths and English in school. Anyway, in holidays the headmaster, he used to give up his time to teach us English and maths. And we had exam, and half of us passed our exams, we were selected to go to, like, technical college.

But because I was healed from that illness, at the healing service, I wanted to be a priest. And the headmaster, Father Brock, said "I will keep you here, until you are ready to go for training." So my father, he said "whatever God wants you to do, you do." And I was like the second person in the school, doing all maintenance, office work, when the headmaster was away, everyone comes to me. I was very happy, I was involved with the church. But after two years, had been a long time waiting. I was then about 20. I didn't want to help in the church. I just felt like I wanted to go on and become a Brother.

Father Brock was like my father. Even my own parents refer to him as my dad, and everybody on the islands know us as like father and son, he looked after me very well. And he was a good friend of Brother Daniel, Franciscan, you know. When I said I wanted to go and join the Franciscans, he got in touch with Brother Daniel, so everything was arranged that way, to the novitiate. All the teachers tried to persuade me to stay, all the boys, really sad to see me go. But I said no, I've got to go.

And I went to the Friary, on a little island. Was beautiful beautiful place, very colourful – was like a little paradise, so still that you could hear all the little birds singing, the frogs singing, the insects. There was one village, probably about 100 people living there. Just the place I wanted to be. I used to get up very early, to pray. And I learned the contemplation, praying that way. That really enriched me. And I was given the responsibility of looking after all the machinery, because I had experience in that. I felt like, you know, I was still doing something that I was used to doing. But one of the things that annoyed me was frogs. In the evenings when we went for Compline, there used to be loads of them, I used to jump like hell, and break silence!

There were three Brothers, about four novices and four or five aspirants and postulants. So is quite a big family. We were more or less self-sufficient, we dried coconut to sell, and we had maybe four cattle. And a piggery, a chicken farm, goats, and grew our own vegetables, and of course go fishing!

I went to Honiara after three years. And Brother Geoffrey sent me to do English. I spoke my own language with my own people, but most language spoken was pidgin English. Is difficult to learn English, you learn it in class and can write it, but everybody will speak pidgin. Honiara, it was big city. I looked at the cars and thought wow! And then when I saw like women driving, that was something! And then I didn't know – why are they not hitting themselves? I never knew that you drive left all the time. And the lights. I mean back home come six o'clock that's it! You have a kind of dry stick with some fire on the end, or dry coconut leaves.

I was there three years. Then Brother Geoffrey got me a place in the nursing school, this was the thing I wanted to do, after I've completed my English course. I was one of the first mature students ever, in the nursing school. So the tutors kept reminding us, you've got to make it so we can take mature students. It was kind of funny, all these youngsters, and me old!

The other thing, the thing I learned while in town was that there is not only the Anglican church, there are other churches as well. Brother Geoffrey used to take me round to show me different churches. At first I didn't want to go in, because I thought it was wrong. One day, he started taking me to the church service, and you know, I thought there's nothing wrong with other churches! And I thought goodness, you know. So my life was kind of opening up.

And then I thought, God has still got bigger plan for me. To go abroad as a missionary – with the Brothers, of course. And I was praying about it. I had no doubt about this. I like to go to New Zealand, for selfish reasons, because my parents have lots of friends in New Zealand, and I always thought the country's so green and beautiful. So I prayed about it – but the Brothers had to decide, and they decided that I should come to Plaistow. So... I welcomed it, you know.

And so I came here. And you know, Honiara it was big, Papua New Guinea was even bigger city, oh, but coming to Manila! Was huge – traffic, and soldiers all round with guns, and things like that! And the hotel was like eight or 12 storeys high. Got to Gatwick, you know, you come out, and you do not walk from the aeroplane to the building! And then I thought we went into a building like this, a room, and it was a train, you know – and we were moving! "This is *strange*!" And the train went into a tunnel, it got all dark, and Brother Geoffrey said "we are underground." Goodness! Please, ground, don't fall on us! I wasn't homesick. I was so excited, this big city, oh my goodness, we used to look at it in magazines, now I am here, it's lovely. And now I can't wait to go back. I miss all the – sea, especially. But – some day. Take the family to see.

I have progressed so much in this place. Brother Julian arranged for me to do adaptation course in nursing. I think the main thing also was, to learn to speak English, because you can't speak pidgin any more here, you know, nobody will understand you. That set me challenges. And I was given three years to stay here. But before the end of the three years, I had left the Community. I had to decide to

What a laugh

The swipe of a knife,
A clean slice and the colour is Red,
The Black one drops dead
and Whites go to supper.

Life to Justice towards
    Century 21.
The gods must be joking.
What a laugh.
                  Joshua

take my Final Vows, or leave. And that was the hardest point in my vocation, because I wasn't really sure. There was that part of me wanted to have a family. I think my parents had a lot of pressure on me. Because I am the only boy in the family, they have land – you know, the custom, the land goes to the men, and the men look after the family, so I have to look after the land for my sisters as well. My parents said, "if you do not get married, might need to sell the land." And so – in the end I decided to leave.

Shortly after I left I met Teresa. I was still living in the Friary, and one of the people who were living here introduced me to St Andrews house group, in Teresa's flat. Teresa had Christopher then. And we began to get more friendly, and we started going out. Went to church together. That was the beginning of the life outside the Franciscan – reintroducing myself to the life outside! It was confusing, because I still very much like to be a Brother. The Brothers were trying to persuade me not to leave, and I didn't want to betray that care and trust, and everything. And then I thought well, maybe I can make a good Christian family. But I don't know whether I have fulfilled that!

It's kind of difficult, because in the Solomons – it's not quite right for England – but the husband is like the head of the family, and the wife listens, you know, to the husband. But me and Teresa find that a bit conflicting. Yesterday, at work I had this feeling, "I got to change". I know it came from God, because it came with a peace of mind, you know, that this is the right thing, I've got to listen, I've got to let Teresa do what she wants with her life. I want to have a good family – and I have – but I want to make it work, so I think I have to listen to that small voice.

I think I've got some things in my life that needs carved off. To mould me to be a better person, more listening and giving! I've been praying as well, a lot. I need change. But I don't know how it will be.

I feel I'm growing more spiritually. I'm not very religious as I used to. But inwardly I'm growing. Even though I hardly go to church, I still pray every day, and I make a prayer with Solomon, and talk about the bible. I know the whole Being, existence, is because of God. Yes. God is life. And strangely, I'm beginning to feel that even the plants, all the creatures in their own language, have their own spirituality maybe. Because the plants, they know the way – if you farm, you know some vines go round this way, they have to go round this way to climb. Others go round this way, you know – I learned that in the village. Yes. So they know.

And if you look at the religions – Islam, you know, Hindu, Buddhist, Christian, yes, Judaism – we all worship same God, which tells me that real life that Jesus promised the Christians is not only found through Christ. For me, I believe what Jesus Christ said. For the Muslim it will be different – that's his belief, what the Prophet that God sent to them, says. I don't think we can limit what God is – can't box him in. God is great and God is in our midst and God is – well, mysterious. Beyond understanding.

Because we are made of earth, we go back to the earth, as water, soil, all minerals, all these come together to form us. Even though we are physically dead and go back to earth, we're back to life, because we make up the earth again. We are made up of, for example, plants. We eat a plant to make us what we are. Then we give back as well, to the earth. So earth is very holy, is our mother, because we are the product of the earth. God took some earth, moulded it, and then gave it life, breath.

In Solomon Islands, it's very holy. I mean, we cut down trees, but there are so many holy places. When you die and are buried, immediately that place that we are buried in become holy, and that's why there's lots of tabu places, because people buried there.

I had a dream about my village. We have this huge tree, in my mother's village. And it's one of the places that people come together. There's church, the custom house, the well. Then there's place for dancing, come together there. A bit like Red Indian dances, you all dance. This big tree has been in my mind for about a year now. Grown so big – and the thing is that, although we kind of respect the land, people have got to survive and they cut down trees or burn them, without thinking.

So anyway, I have been thinking to try and preserve this tree. And I dreamt that I went back, with my family, and we were all going to see that tree. So I looked and it was dying. The tree was dying. People have been cutting some of the roots out and it was dying. And I said, you know, "can still help that tree to survive for another thousand years or something." And then I woke up and wrote a little story about it, more or less like a poem. Saying that this tree has been there for generations and generations, must be a few thousand years old, this tree, and she has seen all the hurricanes, the earthquakes, the droughts and the famines, used to provide shelter and protection for people from giants, you know we have lots of fairy stories that people have come to hide there from the giants. It's kind of given protection.

And I thought maybe I could write to my MP, and try – here we have the Dome, and people and countries are doing different things to celebrate the Millennium, I thought would be a good thing to try and make it to grow for another thousand years. Yes, because after all, even in Christ's time it was already growing. So I think has more right to celebrate the Millennium than us!

Teresa's story

After 14 years in London, Teresa still speaks with the soft lilt of County Cork. Not tall, she is wiry and quick-moving, dark-haired; She doesn't find it easy to tell her story: sometimes the words spill out easily, but generally she feels her way slowly, searching for the words to put round her thoughts.

I was born in Cork City and I grew up in a village in West Cork called Courtmacsherry. I've one sister, Mary, and my mother and my father and my grandmother lived in the house. My grandma was a strong Catholic woman. And my father, he worked as a labourer for farmers or did gardening or one stage he was like a builders' labourer. And so he worked hard. And he used to go to the pub, and he probably increasingly went to the pub as he got older, and worked less.

And my mother was a sacristan and my grandmother before her was a sacristan. She only got like five bob, it was low pay, but I suppose it gave you a status. So she had to ring the Angelus bell at 8 o'clock and open the church, and then at 12 o'clock at the middle of the day it was the Angelus, and then at 6 o'clock. A Monday was the day she cleaned the church. And then there'd be funerals, and my mother would always be there, and my father would ring the bell. There was a harbour, where the sea comes in and out every day, so we're facing the sea, and there's a wood behind, and so you could see when the funeral cars would be coming down the road and my father would start ringing the bell so everyone would know. And everybody came to the funeral.

In the parish there was farmers. But in the summer people came from Cork City on holiday and there was a caravan site and a hotel. And some people had cars so they got jobs in the town, it's ten miles away, and the City, it's 30 miles away, and there's one bus that goes at 8 o'clock in the morning and comes back at five. Our neighbours, there was eight of them, and their mother was English, and they were the type that didn't do their homework much, and they were kind of looked down upon by other people because the mother was English and different, I suppose. And the father, he was a sailor, so he was away a lot, so it was hard for her, really.

I used to go to my friend's house – her mother went to America when she was young, then her husband died so she decided to bring the children back to grow up in the village, so I used to go to their house. I think because they came from outside – for example, I never had a birthday party, but I remember Cathy inviting me to a birthday party, and I thought that was amazing, and she got some presents in the post, and that was – strange. And I remember they used to have a choice of breakfast cereals – I don't know if we had just like porridge or just bread and tea, and I thought that was... And now I think I must have achieved a lot, I've got a choice of breakfast cereals in the morning!

My Nan died, maybe I was ten or something. She used to get bronchitis every winter, and she'd be upstairs and she'd be banging on the floor for my mother to come up and give her a cup of tea, whatever it was. My mother was quiet, she didn't lose her temper or anything, and I think she kind of let my father get away wid things. It was a good job that we were getting the dole, because he wouldn't have given her money, I suppose – he'd go to the pub. And some people, they would go to like a disco in the town, or – it was only an odd time when I'd ask her but she wouldn't let me go. Because she'd be worried, I suppose, because we'd have to thumb a lift.

The priest, he said something once about putting your arms round your father's neck and giving him a kiss. And we were in tears, because we couldn't do that. We weren't good at showing our emotions. But at least they didn't get divorced. It wasn't an option really, but – that could have been worse, I suppose. So I suppose say compared to someone like my friend Maeve, her father was a bank manager, I could say I can't expect to be as good or whatever it is. But in a way he was a bit powerless, I mean he had to work hard. He said that once. You know, weeding the crops or whatever you had to do in those days, and now they have more machines. So he wasn't really skilled in anything.

And I think there was a kind of a conflict in me, because being religious we all had to go to confession regularly, and one thing was respect your parents, honour your father and your mother and I suppose sometimes I used to think well I didn't respect my father. And he prided himself on saying "well I've never laid a finger on my two girls" – and in a way maybe he should have disciplined us more. Obviously we've none of us got perfect parents, and we – I expect it depends on how much we're pushed to do things, to persevere, that we achieve in our lives.

I feel like I grew away when I went to university. My mother kept saying, she wanted me to get a job. She used to say to me, I should do home economics, like, and learn to cook. And she was right, actually. And I suppose she didn't really show me how to cook. In a way, she didn't explain. So I think you could say she was getting old, because she married when she was about 39, I think. Cause I remember my mother saying she could have been a nurse, but she stayed at home to look after my grandmother.

My mother died of cancer when I was 20, and nobody really spoke about what it was. And my father, he can probably write because he learned at school, but he never did any writing. And I think he wasn't that sympathetic to my mother when she was in a lot of pain. It was my sister that was better. She had got married young, at 17. And my sister was there wid her a lot and realised how bad she was deteriorating.

I'm glad I went to a convent school. There was some nuns that were teachers and there were some lay teachers. It was a good influence, like. And then there was an art teacher and she was good, and I think the science – there were some young nuns. One of them, Sister Michael, she used to play volley-ball – they won the All-Ireland Volleyball. And when I went into the Catholic church, there's like a reverence, because God's presence is there, and it's not found in other maybe church buildings which are just thought of as buildings.

I studied social science, I wanted to be a social worker. You know, it was a change for one of my family to go to university. I got a grant, £1,000, and like I wouldn't have got any money from my father, I suppose. But I mean in Ireland, it's full of undergraduates, you know, they think that education is very important.

I remember this girl, Maeve, she kind of adopted me when we went to university. She invited me to a meeting, so I went, and the people were Catholics, I don't know if they were practising, but they were saying, you know, "invite Jesus into your life", and eventually I did. And I suppose I half believed it, because it was written in the bible, but I didn't think I hadn't been a Christian before. I remember once, one of the boys saying he wasn't going to Mass any more, and I was kind of shocked. But when I came to England, I missed the fellowship, so I found a Baptist church and I used to go to Mass on a Sunday morning and go to the evening service there, and eventually I stopped going to Mass, and didn't feel guilty about it. And eventually I got baptised in the Baptist church. But I don't think even my sister can understand why I'm not Catholic. I'd like to talk to a priest, to see how much – I think they've become a bit more open now, as regards to sin and all this.

My mother died when I was in the third year of university, and then in the July, there was only my father living in the house then, and my cousins came

Birth

Birth is but one stage in the cycle of reluctance that we call life. From outswimming the competition of conception to the failure to come to terms with inevitable death. Birth is just our first struggle against the changes that life holds for all of us.

The woman is in labour, but this baby is not coming out without a fight. At last he is born. Everyone is happy. Everyone is laughing. Laughing at him. He hates the bitterness of defeat. But they're not through with him yet. Insult is added to injury. He is slapped about, he has his head squeezed. Unfortunately, he is a bad loser. He takes it without grace and cries in protest. But no one is listening. No one understands.

He decides to urinate all over the nurses and just for a moment tastes how sweet revenge can be. His victory is short-lived. Retaliation comes swiftly and brutally. In one stroke he is severed from his mother's womb. He quickly realises how unforgiving people can be.

The pain he feels is unbearable. 'Stop, stop,' is all he wants to say, but doesn't know how. If only he could speak English.

Izzy

over from England and I decided to go back wid them. I stayed wid my aunt in Richmond, then I got a job as a care assistant in a home. And in a way I wish I'd kept in touch wid some of the girls in my university and come to London wid them. When I used to go home, at Christmas, you meet other people that you knew, and that's nice, all these Irish people. I did meet some people in the home where I was living, and they used to play music, and I went to one or two things wid them. People say that they don't think of Irish people as very different from English, not like other immigrants, but I do feel like an immigrant sometimes. And I suppose, it's just the difference between rich and poor. And Ireland – in a way, it is a rural country, and this is the city.

I think when the IRA were bombing, some of the English didn't like the Irish, but I don't really experience that. But I think people don't know, in England, how much Irish people didn't like English people in the past, because of the English occupation of Ireland and that. I mean some Irish people obviously don't want the English to still be in the Six Counties, but I think the English have put a lot of money into the Six Counties, so... I mean, if you're Irish you do feel a bit of patriotism, when you think that there was people in 1922 gave their lives for freedom and now we're a Republic. And Irish language, nobody knows much about it here, but in Ireland it's like the road signs are in Irish and in English, and people, if they can afford it, might send their children to the Gaeltacht, to learn Irish during the summer holidays. And there's Irish games, and Irish music. So that's nice, it's important.

I tried nurse training in Kingston hospital, and then they thought I wasn't really cut out for it, so then I did some agency care assistant work. And then I saw a job as a resident social worker in a children's home in Newham. And I applied, even though I didn't know where it was, or anybody. So I decided to come over here in about '89, I think, and I lived in a shared house. And then I got pregnant wid Christopher. I went back to work part time after my maternity leave, I lived in staff accommodation. And then when I came back after maternity leave wid Solomon I was redeployed as a team clerk in Stratford, and then I left nearly three years ago now.

When I came to Newham, I started going to the Elim Pentecostal church, and that's where I met Christopher's dad, because he went to a Ghanaian church that met in the same – the Elim Ghanaian church. Then when I was going to St Andrews church, I had a home group in my house, and Oliver came. We married three years ago now.

When I was working, I used to think, well, I'm achieving, I'm balancing the budget, say when I was on my own wid Christopher, I felt that that was an achievement. There are benefits, money benefits from the government, but it may be an achievement for somebody like me to not get them, you know.

And obviously there's a pressure in life to achieve and to earn. If you work you have some independence and money. But I was looking at a girl who was a secretary, and I thought, she's got a child, she takes her to school, she comes to work, she collects her child from home, she makes her dinner, and I thought is that really what I want from life? But it's getting a balance between working too hard and feeling you're not achieving anything. Well, I'm actually enjoying not working, and I know that there's a lot of voluntary work possible, for people that stay at home. And I was thinking, wid St Phillips. – this area there's lots of flats, council houses, and there could be a need for some social activities, but you need obviously to bring your vision across to other people. And obviously the difficulty of doing anything is working together. But I am happy when there's people around, like at my wedding, I thought that was a good opportunity to bring people together. And I think that's good. Sometimes when I used to go to church in Richmond, I used to think, oh isn't this nice, if the sun was shining and we were all going to worship.

But part of maybe me feeling that I'd like to do something in this community is because I've had experience of some problems of families here from working in the children's home. Like there was a boy that came for one night, he was on police bail and they had to put him somewhere so he'd turn up in court next day. And he ran away, and I could understand why, he'd never bin to the place before. And I can see like a teenager, I mean life isn't what you'd want for them anyway.

Before you have children, it doesn't seem to matter if you're Catholic or what you are. But now in a way I feel a bit sorry that I'm not. I tried to get Christopher into the Catholic school but because he's not christened he can't. And there's not many Church of England schools. Like if it was Catholic he'd be learning the catechism for your first communion, and I think he'd be learning more, in a way, of religion. I mean I know it's up to me as well, to teach it. But inner city London, it's not a religious environment, much, unless we make it one.

I think going to confession is actually a good thing, it pulls you up every so often. You have to say to God you're sorry for your sins, but it's hard to say, every few weeks you have to take time to go through them, and think how often have I done that, and that. And it's humbling, and I feel that when you grow up you can be less humble, accepting of things. And sometimes like I say things to people that hurt them – like judging them as to what I think things should be. And maybe I'll apologise, but the problem might be still there, the issue.

We're going to Ireland in half term. I went wid Christopher when he was small, and then Solomon hasn't been yet, or Oliver, so we're going to go. But first of all I don't know if my brother-in-law wanted Oliver to come, because he – being black, it's a big difference. Even my sister was a bit worried about what people would say. I wasn't worried, but she was. In Cork City, in university, you get some African students, or doctors, Indians and that, but not much in the countryside. When I took Christopher over, they thought he was a Romanian orphan, because people at the time were adopting Romanian orphans.

My mother wouldn't've expected me to marry a – because I remember when we came on holiday, my mother and me and my sister, she saw these little girls wid their pigtails, you know, and she said "look at the way they're doing their hair, they're trying to be more white!" You know, she had this thought that they'd be better off white, kind of thing. I mean, there was a girl who went to Trinity College in Dublin, and she met a Nigerian guy and married him and had two children, and they came to my village to visit their grandmother, and I was friends wid them, and I thought they were great, because they were different, you know. But there aren't many people of other races in rural Ireland.

When I was at university, I was fascinated by campaigns – say, you mightn't buy oranges from Israel, because there was a boycott. And it was all a way of life to an extent, that we were supposed to be helping the poor, or maybe go on marches against the Bomb. And there's a whole world of things you can be involved in. I'd like my children to be aware – concern for the underdog, I suppose you could say. A concern for injustice. I suppose you're identifying yourself as something rather than something else. It's a case of making your voice heard, I expect. The idealism – it gives you something to work towards, away from the everyday. I mean it's the idea that people can take control of their lives and think about why they're poor, and examine – a whole new world!

But people don't like change, you know – you need some motivation!

Claire's story

Claire is a very private person. She told me her story, and it was beautiful. As I listened and then read it through, it sang in my head like music. It was a song of love. But she did not want it to be known in such detail, and so she wrote it for me, briefly, together with the story of how she first met the Brothers in Balaam Street: that, to her, seemed more important. Claire speaks simply, her voice lilting; sometimes it's filled with laughter, sometimes with tears. When she speaks of people who have been good to her, it is filled with warmth and wonder. Her small terraced home is very peaceful. There is pottery that she has made and painted herself; plants and dried flowers; and, above the fireplace, pictures of Jesus, the Sacred Heart, Sacré Coeur.

I come from India from a colony where we were speaking French. When I was still a child we went on pilgrimage to a place, a little village where at that time there was no bus running. An insignificant village, where Our Lady appeared to a little boy who was lame. She had a baby in her arms. She asked to build a chapel there. Later, Portuguese sailors were in danger at sea and prayed Our Lady that a chapel will be built if they were saved. They did so beause it was at that place they landed.

During the feast, the pilgrimage, there was an epidémie of cholera and my mother contracted it and died. I was taken by a nun my mother asked to look after me if something happens to her. This nun put me in a convent where I was taken care and with other children till the age of 11. I was happy and went to school like other children. Later I suffered a great deal at the hand of this headmistress who was not good, for four years. I was taught to do needlework that I hated. Always in tears and punished every day.

During my childhood a nun called Mother Louise was a mother to me and taught me to pray. My love for God has kept me all these years.

At the age of 15 I asked to be a nun but was told that I have to wait till 19. In the novitiate I fell from the stairs, injured my back. I left the convent and helped in the Catholic Movement for young children. I was a Dirigeante with lots of responsibilities. Devoted myself to this work.

Later I got married and had four children, all married now with their own families. We live in London now from 1962. Many people left India when Independence came.

At present I live alone and I try the best I can to love God and spend time in prayer. It does not mean that I sit and pray, but by everything I do I make it a prayer to the God who loves me and makes me feel His presence. So close to me, giving me strength to carry on, at every moment, sometimes in darkness. I know His hands are always there comforting me. He is my only hope and love till the time when I will go and meet Him face to face.

I do not remember exactly the year I went to the Friary to find out about the Franciscan Brothers who live at 42 Balaam Street. I wanted to write about their life in the Order.

I used to see them walking near the Friary, the Brown Brothers, who reminded me of St Francis or St Anthony leaving everything to live with the poor and help them.

As I was trying to learn a little bit more about the English language, I went to a course. I chose to write about the Franciscan Brothers.

I went into the Friary for the first time to ask the Brother in charge if he could give me a rendez-vous. Brother Julian received me and took me to the chapel and the garden. I felt this peace and silence like a mantle covering me. It was a strange feeling, like entering a shrine, a place of prayer. The whole place was telling you to respect and tread carefully. I

The garden at 42

could not help telling Brother Julian what I felt. I said this peace, seems a place of prayer. You could feel them through the years, those Brothers walking in the garden saying their prayers.

I felt strange there. Brother Julian told me, come any time you wish.

I started going once a month and spend the day in silence in the little chapel, join them at midday prayer. Though the Friary is only a few streets away from where I live, it was like I went a long way from home. You felt completely lost in prayer in that little chapel, that invites you to silence and fills you with peace.

I still go there, after so many years. The Friary is a place of silence, peace and prayer. Surely I have received many graces there.

Alan's story

Alan is of medium height, squarely built. He speaks, as he moves, rather heavily. Yet when he smiles, as he does often, his face lights up, warm and interested. His voice is low and gravelly, becoming inflected only when something moves him – gratitude or a memory of joy. There's strength in him, immovable: he follows his own paths, within the boundaries he's accepted for himself.

I was born the 21st of April 1959. My twin sister, Susan – I popped out first, she followed. But the first seven years of our lives, Susan and I were in Dr Barnardos in Essex.

My mum was living at that time with her mother in Custom House. Later, we lived in a three-bedroomed flat in Canning Town, you didn't have a kitchen, it was a scullery, and coal cupboard, there was dripping dampness on the walls. And there was only one coal fire. No hot water – we always had to wash in, it was called the scullery, my mum had to use a bowl, because people didn't use their baths, they used to fill them up with coal because it was too expensive.

I was about 12 months when my natural father left. The other shock was that my stepfather's marriage to my mother was bigamous, which she didn't know. And he had about nine children by the first wife. My mum had nine children, but two died in infancy. They were together for about two years and then when she fell pregnant, he abandoned her, so she went out to work as an orderly in Poplar. She was like supporting my twin sister and myself, and my gran. Those were the days when you didn't get as much welfare support.

And I've got really blissful memories of Barnardos, like those six, seven years were really blissful. It was like a little village, about eight, nine children in each house, and I used to go and visit all my friends on my bicycle. I went to this Infants' school, and I can remember that I used to ring the bell at breaktime. And there was a boy there that I was really fond of, when I told him I was leaving, I can remember really being upset. But I think to myself, maybe that's why I'm so sane today, because the first seven years are the formative years, and fortunately I got lots of love and care. Because even when I was like psychotic, there was still a thread of sanity in the background. Like a thread there that wouldn't break.

When I left Barnardos, I think – I suffered a lot of mental, psychological abuse from my stepfather. He rejected me because I was the child of my mum's lover, and I was half-Pakistani. He was just really really racist. He used to call me Wog, and he used to say to my mother "get that Paki out of my my front room," you know. And I've got very low self-esteem, and it's almost like that voice haunts me.

And my mum couldn't really cope, cos we were in crowded, insanitary conditions, three or four in one bedroom. And stepfather was having affairs with other women, and he'd sling my mother out, and she used to like end up physically abusing me, but it was because she couldn't cope.

And then when I was 11, I was really unhappy, and I became a bit delinquent. And then my twin sister, she wasn't getting enough love, she started to sleep with lorry drivers. So in the end she was committed back into local authority care. And one day, I must have stolen like a calculating machine, and then I was prosecuted. So then I ended up in what they call an Observation and Assessment Centre. I was there for about a year, then they just decided that best thing was to go to a children's home. A thing that really upset me, because I've always like doubted my intelligence and gifts, was that they wrongly assessed me as mentally subnormal. And then an educational psychologist, after about six months, she reassessed me, she said "if anything, Alan's of good, upper average intelligence," and my reading level was way ahead of my age. And I used to take refuge in books, and when I was a teenager I used to chain-read. I think I burnt myself out by just reading. Because by the time I got to 19, 20, years old, I had a nervous breakdown – I got really depressed, because I couldn't read. But I managed to leave school with some CSEs and a couple of O' levels.

I used to go over to Wanstead Flats, birdwatching. And in summer I could hear the skylarks singing, and I used to wish that I could find the nest, and I just jumped for joy, because I was observing this skylark, and all of a sudden I found this little hole in the ground, and there were four eggs, and I just jumped for joy, because they're so hard to find.

When I was in the children's home I met my auntie Sylvia. She was a kind of social aunt – they get approval from Social Services. And we were really close, and she stimulated an interest in like the arts, and she used to take us camping. And she rings me every couple of weeks, she just said to me, "you're an important part of my life."

And the other person that is very significant to me is my godmother, Rachel Warden. She really helped me. I used to go to her house, and then when I was diagnosed as manic depressive, she used to visit me – she was doing a 72 hour week as a GP, she used to drive all the way from Billericay. She helped me to understand my psychosis. Because I was very very angry, and she used to make me aware of what I was doing, so that I'm in control of my destructive tendencies.

I think if I compare myself to other people who suffer from manic depression, I do really well, within my limitations. But sometimes I think, if I didn't have this affliction, my life would not be quite so limited. I try not to think along those lines, because I don't want to make myself discontented. But I would have like to have been a lawyer. I did work for a solicitor when I left school, and then I went to night school and I did an O' level in law and English language, and then I tried to do some A' levels, but

> **The locked ward**
>
> There's no hope on the locked ward
>   There's no soap on the locked ward
> They give you no rope on the locked ward
> Everyone a sheer dear queer dope
>   on the locked ward
> So hear me hippy man barefoot brown hippy girl
> if you really can't cope
> you'll finish up in our
>   locked ward
> The locked ward, ah locked ward
> The locked ward!
>
> John the Buddhist

I had to abandon the course, because I'd started to develop the illness. I had a flat at Stratford, and I was doing law, politics, government and history. But then I got really despairing, and I OD'd, overdosed, a couple of times.

And I was found wandering along the A13 in a psychotic state, like I was crying, throwing bits of wood at the motorway, and then they said to me, "it's best for you, you voluntarily agree to go into Goodmayes," so I did, cos I didn't want to be sectioned. Oh, I hated it. Because I was really confused. I wasn't really told where I was going. And when I got there, it was this horrible institution.

One thing I really hate about psychiatric hospitals is that once you're in, nobody really listens to what you say, all you say is like fantasy. I just think that's wrong. You're robbed of your rights as a citizen, in a sense. I mean, even today, I have this fear of authority, because in hospital they're constantly observing you and writing a daily – it's almost like "he's been a good boy today, or a bad..." So when the next shift come on, it's ike when daddy comes home from work, he hears from mummy that you've not been behaving nicely, he'll be really like stern with you.

After I came back to Plaistow, it took me quite a long time to adjust. I had to move into a psychiatric hostel. And oh, it reminded me of bedlam. It was supposed to be a half-way house. And I couldn't afford clothes or anything. Cos when you have to live on state benefits, you can't – you know, it's like a decent pair of shoes cost thirty pounds. It's really hard, you know. It made me feel a bit like a leper. Even now, I always say to people, pretend that I'm working. Because people despise you. Not all people, but there's a lot of people that just think you're a scrounger..

And so in the end, I just thought well I've had enough. So I just broke into my old flat, and I refused to budge. And then after I got it legally sorted out that I could stay there, I felt I had my autonomy again. In the sense that you didn't have someone saying "come on Alan, you've got to go to a day centre."

Anyway, in the end my flat-mates moved out, and I was in a three-bedroomed flat, which I did start to find really hard. And I was having a lot of problems with some thugs in the area. Because I was basically a polite person, if I was going through the park, pass people, say "excuse me," and they used to take the piss, and say "oh excuse me!" and I'd be spat at. And they could see – because I wasn't very well, you could tell, and they used to take the piss, really. I did have friends, but my family had moved to Dagenham, my mum was nursing a sick husband as well as looking after two disabled sisters, she couldn't – she still is now, you know, looking after two disabled – she's 61 now.

So in the end, I went to Social Services, and the duty officer said, "oh Alan," she said, "there's a Brother that's just set up Helping Hands, and I think he'd be really grateful for someone with typing skills." So then Brother Julian invited me to come and have lunch. I really hated myself, and I was just going around in rags, because I couldn't afford – and when I came to the Friary, one of the wonderful things was that Julian used to say, "go up to the jumble room and help yourself," and often really nice things – it was really nice to have a bit more dignity, you know.

But I did come to the Friary. And I used to pray, like, to God, I said, "oh I wish I had more brothers and sisters,' and a bit later on, I thought God! that prayer was answered. Cos it was like all the Brothers and Sisters became like my extended family. And Julian was really like a guardian to me. He helped me to undo a lot of the judgemental Christianity that I'd absorbed. I always had this fear that I was a bad person, would go to hell.

But I was living down Grange Road, and oh, it was horrible down there. I was occupying a three-bedroom on my own, I was in a strong position to negotiate with my Housing Association, for a one bedroom. So that's what I did, and I'm now living in Maud Road, and I've turned it into a really cosy little home. I'm a home-maker, and I've made it quite palatial, Julian calls me a "pauper living in a palace"! I've never had a bedroom of my own, it's only since I've been an adult that I've had my own bedroom.

Being gay? I remember when I was in the children's home in my late teens, having the feelings, but just feeling really ashamed and guilty, and I used to wish that those feelings would go, but I found they strengthened. But I didn't actually come out to myself till I was about 30. And then I had my first, like proper boyfriend relationship when I was 32. And that lasted for about a couple of years. But I'm very wary now about getting into a relationship. Because I know that when I did get hurt, that I changed, I became very spiteful. It was horrible. Cos it is true that you can only hate someone who you first love.

But I've reinvented my life now, and I do a bit of voluntary cleaning, gives me a bit of pocket money, and I'm just happy, really. So long as I'm making a tiny contribution, I'm quite happy. Actually, I see this illness now as an asset, because I could be doing some soul-destroying job, whereas I've got full autonomy – I'm just free, really.

I think what makes me really happy is being able to enjoy my music. Because basically I'm creative, I do like music, it puts me in touch with my emotional side. I started going clubbing, and I really do like dancing. And I enjoy being with younger people, who are vibrant and full of energy. And I like to squeeze an odd bottom when I can get away with it! And I like the night life. Most of the population is asleep, you come back on the night bus, see London all lit up. And then you see like people cleaning the BT telephone kiosks and people sweeping the streets, and you see people on the buses that you wouldn't normally see.

I mean I am a little bit materialistic, but amassing lots of money and things isn't important to me. Spirituality, I think that it makes you care more for other people and animals. I wouldn't want to be obsessed with material things and nothing else, I like the two to complement each other. And it gives me the hope that all the things that happened to me, there may be some reason that I'll discover in the later life. Kind of a preparation.

I prefer to call myself a spiritual person rather than a religious. I don't want to be bound by teachings. I can see a lot of prejudice in the writings of the bible. I know we're all guilty of doing it, but I don't want to become one of these intolerant – judging other people, trying to play God. Coming to the Friary, it made me realise that Christians can have different beliefs. And can disagree as well! I believe that, like the Quakers do, in all things. I don't feel that God's gonna judge me if I don't go to church, cos it's your heart, and you can be thinking and praying wherever you are.

I often feel as though God's got me in his hand, you know – I often thank God for the people I've met today. And very often I'm just lying in bed, and I'm just like basking in God's presence – you're lying there, and the next thing you're in a really nourishing, deep sleep. It's really nice. Like this afternoon, John came over and we listened to music, aand then as soon as I said goodbye to John, I felt as though – maybe it's God – you know, there in the presence of both of us. It's a hard thing to explain. Or even something of God that was in John, you know, that came to me. But I used to say to Julian, "it's like St Paul said, that nothing can separate us from the love of God." And I said, "if he knew what some of these depressions were like, would he be able to say that?" Cos you feel so cut off, it really made

> **Identity (we and they)**
>
> I belong to, We are
> and They are such.
> We, therefore, SUPERIOR.
>
> I belong to, We are
> and Oppressed by superiors.
> But to our gods we cry,
> the afterlife our reward.
> We shall therefore be superior!
>
> *Joshua*

you think that there was no love, no hope, no nothing. Like the depths of depression were just like a fog – that God's love couldn't penetrate through it.

Now, I live in the present really, not because I'm afraid, but I think you can waste so much time, we can spend so much time either looking to the past or being concerned with the future, and it's the present that's ticking by. It's like now that counts.

I'm really close to Mum. It's taken about 17, 18 years, it's still going on, but it's like reconciliation and healing. It's not till you have hindsight and adult understanding – I can see now that my mum struggled, that she's always loved us, and she struggled, it's just that she had so many odds against her. I think being reconciled to my family, trying to break the chain, so that the anger doesn't continue into the next generation, then I can feel like when I die, that I did something of value.

But I really do like Newham. I wouldn't want to live anywhere else. I wouldn't like to live in Canning Town or Custom House, they're like – you've got high crime, you know. And they're very depressing. You know, cos they tend to be concrete jungles, and all these sort of horrible estates. And I grew up in those areas when I was a kid, and I just... And you've got the A13, it cuts right through the borough, and people who live in Custom House, it's like you're cut off from the rest of the borough. And there was the Ronan Point, the gas explosion, two of my relatives were killed in that explosion. Yeah. Long time ago. Plaistow, it's where all my friends are, I feel really rooted here. And I always feel accepted here, at the Friary. I feel valued. I'm Alan, and that's all that matters. It doesn't matter whether I'm gay or what, it's irrelevant, I'm just me.

But I feel old! I do! Oh, I feel as if I've got an old head on young shoulders. It's as though I wish I could've been allowed to have bin a child. I wish that I could be more frivolous. Yes, if I could have a wish, it would be that I could smile more spontaneously, like I used to. Hopefully, by the time the undertaker puts me in the grave, there'll be a big smile on my face before they put on the lid! Nail on the lid!

Childhood memories of blackened grates and ash-strewn hearths. Ebony clods of fluffy soot spatter down and shower the fireside rug. Sheets cover floor and furniture when the chimney sweep calls. Rod upon rod join together, then the round black whiskers of the brush crown the lengthy pole. We must run, quickly, to the end of the garden so that we can shout to the sweep, "Yes!" when a cloud of soot puffs from the chimney pot and his brush waves in the heavens.

Paper, then wood, then coal – one match setting a little flame to the paper, charring then, zestful, spreading until all was afire. Glowing red and gold. Some days, the flame died young as the draught blew strong down the chimney opening. Patient coaxing, perhaps a last-ditch attempt with a sheet of newspaper held over the chimney opening to help draw the flames upwards, accompanied by untold mutterings, especially if the sheet itself caught fire.

Toasting feet before the warmth of the fire. Hot toast browned by the fiery glow; potatoes in their jackets tucked under the grate – those tasty, ash-covered skins... Chestnuts roasting, and exploding; indoor fireworks...

"Pictures" in the fire. Lazing in a cosy chair, gazing at the dancing flames and hot coals, all sorts of images... The sounds of fire – whispering, fluttering, hissing; the tumble of coal or log sending up a shower of crackling sparks. Light dancing on faces and furniture, a rosy glow of warmth, comfort and security. The shadows, dark and sombre, driven into the background by the living flames.

If you were ill, a fire in the usually empty bedroom fireplace. Eiderdown wrapped snugly; warm inner glow from hot bread and milk; eyes drooping into slumber as the fire sings and the shadows dance.

And... coldly cleaning up the grate each morning; going out into inches of snow to fill up the coal scuttle. Feet were warm in front of the fire, but the back could be like an iceberg. Hot water from the coke-burning boiler in the kitchen – if it was in a good mood. Should the wind veer to the north-east or Dad decide to bank the boiler up with hedge clippings, well... Smoke billowed everywhere, eyes cascaded tears. The washing, airing in the kitchen, stank like Guy Fawkes.

Friend Roger still puts logs on an open fire. The cat dreamily gazes with amber eyes as the flames flicker and dance. And so too do I and my companions, as fire weaves its spell.

Joan

Tom's story

Tom, tall and squarely built, speaks fast, often in a tone of discovery. He does not seem to live in the past, but firmly in the present, always self-aware, always looking at the significance of what is happening. Yet the past, its scents and sounds and atmosphere, and especially those few outstanding people who have most influenced him, are very real as he speaks. They've helped to make him who he is. Tom is Chair of Helping Hands.

I was born on 25th September 1964 at Whitehaven General Hospital in Cumbria. My father was a civil engineer, and he always wanted to be a policeman in London. So at the age of five, I – my sister hadn't come along then – and my mum and dad moved down to London. I can remember where we were, fondly, it was at the Spotted Dog near West Ham Park. It was a happy time for me – an adventure, because we'd just come down from Cumbria. Cumbria's a bit of a blur, but I remember going in the fields, running after my dad's crossbow bows. I probably thought I was doing something exciting, doing something with my dad.

My dad was very busy, so I didn't see him that much. I liked my own company. I have a vivid imagination, so that used to stand me in good stead. And I was interested in soldiers and things like that. I used to hide in my room for hours and wait for my dad to come up the stairs, used to run out and greet my dad. And then we moved to Plaistow. It was a lovely road, all police houses, everyone knew each other. Again I kept myself to myself, although we had very good neighbours, so it was a joy to be there. Dad was busy, and Mum was looking after us two.

Then I went to school, Southern Road Infants school. That was an enjoyable time. Went through that very quickly. Then went to Secondary school, probably not much to say about that. It went very quickly. I enjoyed history, English, PE, but I was very bad at maths and sciences. I'm still very bad at maths, I think that's probably why I gave up with a lot of things. At 17 I went to join the army, the Grenadier Guards. I didn't serve my full term, did five years.

I think my problem was, I think too much. And when you think too much you don't make a good soldier, because you question certain things. It's an easy life, do as you're told and everything else is available. And I knew I didn't want that, but then I shouldn't be in the army. It's as simple as that.

I think deep down I'm quite sensitive, so it's difficult. When the Gulf war happened, I would not have fought, but Kosovo – it's funny. You've still got part of the military programming. Although I'm an individual and I'd question orders, when I see what happens out there, I still feel it would be just to go there and if necessary fight and if necessary kill someone, to stop what's going on. And I've got two children, and I believe you can't just sit there and hope sometimes that things are gonna go away.

There was one incident which deeply affected me. There was a young boy who was the only survivor of his family in Kosovo. His whole family were shot, including his sisters and brothers. The Serbians burnt the house. And his little sister was crying for him to help her and he wasn't strong enough. And I probably would go, if – I saw Sean and Stephen in that young boy.

Anyway, I bought myself out. I was about 26. I didn't know what job I was gonna do. I was panicking.

There was about six months I was unemployed, which was quite harrowing. I've never bin unemployed before, it's very degrading. And you could get in a rut. I was quite lucky, my dad arrested someone at Sainsburys, a butcher, and he come home and said "do yourself a favour, go and see if there's a job going." And they put me on a four-week course, and there I was, a butcher. So I plodded away for about a year, living at home. I was saving and saving, I knew I needed to travel. I didn't know where, though.

And I was at Sainsburys, and one of the cleaners was cleaning the meat room, and when he was finished we would go for a beer. And we was listening to Dire Straits, and he said "oh, this reminds me of Israel." And he explained about working in the fields and the orange groves – and I knew that that's where I'm gonna go. So I went back the next day and gave three months notice. Thinking what have I done? I'm gonna go on my own, I didn't know where to go.

I went to the library, got a book about kibbutz. It says there's a place called the Kibbutz Representatives. They booked me, I told Mum and Dad, I think they just thought I had one of my funny ideas, cos I used to come out with funny ideas every five minutes, probably didn't take it that seriously till my air ticket arrived.

And it was one of the best feelings I've had in my life. I knew I had to escape, I had to find out about life, and I needed to be on my own. Normally it's in my imagination, but this was gonna be real. As we taxied out and took off, it was so intense, everything was left behind me and I knew I had to just get on with being Tom Nixon. It was a really good feeling. And first morning at the kibbutz, five o'clock they woke us up, this extreme heat, woodpigeons cooing and goats farting and snorting, and we didn't know all these sounds. And I opened my door, and I was in Shangri La. I was in this fertile, green, in the middle of the Negev desert. It was irrigated by the Kibbutzniks. So that was it.

They gave me the best job I've ever had, with the goats. I had four dogs, two sheep dogs and two Bedouin dogs. So you'd go out four, five miles, and you'd put your little shelter up, get your radio, got the water. And there might be a bit of trouble now and then, so you go and sort that out, your dogs are happy by your side.

It was probably the most happiest I've been in my life. All the army stuff, the doubts and the nightmares. I had 400 therapists all squirting and farting and looking at me. And I had four friends, four little dogs who understood me but didn't go on all the time, I used to talk to them sometimes. So they're probably thinking "yeah well, Tom, you'll be okay, just give it another six months and see what happens." So I done that. Just taking goats out and taking goats back. And it just flew by, that time.

And I made a silly mistake. My friend Michael wanted to go back home, so I said "oh I'll come back with you." Very quickly, went back again. Straight back to the kibbutz, straight to the goats.

But I didn't work too long with the goats. I was sent into the butchers. It was a bit unpleasant, but I got on well with a big German, Boris. Boris was about 78. I couldn't speak German or Hebrew, and he couldn't speak English, but we had a lot in common. He had like a disability, because they took a leg bone out of his leg and swopped it with an arm bone as an experiment in the concentration camps. He only survived because he was so strong. It was important to me to spend a bit of time with Boris. We didn't have a bloody clue what we were saying to each other. We'd sit there for maybe two hours, and we didn't talk. But I think we communicated in our own way. Then Boris died.

I was moved to the kitchen. My saviour there was the cook, Heskie. He was the lawyer for the whole kibbutz movement. When people join the kibbutz, you give up all your wealth, so you come with no baggage. I love that – no one's above anyone else. Heskie was very very clever man. We struck up this very good friendship. And I think that's where I got my taste for law, representing people and doing your best, winning arguments. Because I used to listen to him intensely, and thinking – that's how I think. And one evening, he gave me the key to his house – it was very moving. It was almost like another family. That gesture, I'll never forget.

I went to another kibbutz. Got my heart broken by a beautiful Israeli called Vered, so I left, on my own. I think you should, at times like that. I went back to Kibbutz Lahav. It gets worse, though! There was an American girl there, we spent time together. But she had to go back to America. And I didn't know what to do. It was too soon after Vered. It's funny, in England, I've never had this sense of pain. It's almost – I've never bin stabbed in the heart – and I don't mean in the romantic sense, I mean literally feeling… I just didn't know what to do.

A friend of mine had a place in the Arava desert, that's the hottest part of Israel. It was great, therapeutic. I was at my peak of fitness. You work hard and you play hard, it's a rough environment, but it's great. Then I heard of a mosh'av called Faran. And I went to a party and I met Sue. She was from Finland, and we got on really well and then like became a couple. It was getting a bit silly then, because when you're working in that close group of men and you meet someone, you don't fit in.

So we went to a place right near the Jordanian border, beautiful view. And they had a manmade oasis, with a waterfall and all that stuff. But volunteers done all the minor repairs. It was like a place for families to go, in the middle of the desert. Such a cushy number, it was uncanny. I used to visit Sue once, twice a week. We worked really hard. And then my visa was running out, and I told Sue we needed to think about coming back to England. I wasn't looking forward to it. I just didn't want to go home. It was horrible. That's where my life changed completely.

Got a job butchering. Sue was living at home, and we needed our own place. I found out there was a school caretaker's job at the Council, I didn't really know anything about the Council, I just knew it was a good job. We went into a house in Kingsland Road, very good money, saving away. And the opportunity come for a residential caretaker, it was an opportunity to have our own place. So I'm a full-fledged council worker, wife's expecting a baby, we've got a three-bedroomed place. At that time, it's enough, I'm happy. Thinking okay – this was September '88ish – I haven't done too bad, I've been away for a while, I don't like being back home, but I've got to make the best of it now.

Sue went back to nursing. I heard there was an opening for a shop steward. I thought what's that? Someone who opens their mouth a lot. So I thought well, I can do that. Didn't know that much about unions, heard a bit from my grandad and how important unions were. But I'd never experienced unions. So I thought I may as well make a name for myself, and mouth off a bit, and it paid off in a way. I think I was quite a good shop steward, I got things done and people trusted me. So I thought what happens after shop steward, what do I do? My predecessor told me there was a position for a branch chairperson. He said "all you got to do is open your mouth a bit more." Oh, I can do that, I'm thinking, this is all right, this.

I got voted in, I was really really lucky. It normally happens over 20 years. It just so happened the guy was retiring, and I suppose I was technically the most prominent shop steward. And I suppose my predecessor thought he could use me, to do all the shouting for him. But I didn't care, cos I thought I'm gonna have your job when you go. I suppose it was like for like, in a way. So in the space of a year I was shop steward and a branch chair, and I'm thinking I can't be that lucky – well, within two years, I'd become a branch secretary. Cos he was retiring. And now I'm the branch secretary for Newham. I've been doing it for four years.

You don't realise what you're letting yourself in for. If you're not supported, it's very daunting, lonely – which doesn't bother me. Because you can't be friends with everyone, you've got to be just as determined and strong for everyone. I think people understand me now, but obviously they can't understand how easy it is for me to switch off and be on my own, and then switch back on again when I'm needed.

For the last year, I've been going through a bit of a difficult time where my colleagues and I were almost being persecuted by a councillor who thought we had the audacity to stand against the Labour Party. What's I suppose a bit annoying for me, is that I think we've forgotten why we did it. We're all worried about compensation now, and "pain and suffering". But we did this because we wanted to keep open the elderly Homes, and the Council were denying that they were gonna close them. And they have closed them. So it wasn't really a political thing, we were just trying to tell them we don't agree with what you're doing, and you're lying to us. And history now has proven that. And in reality, if we were to get one elderly Home opened back up, that would be probably more substantial than what we're expecting. Because that's not why we did it. We just thought we'd remind them, and constantly tell them that what you're doing is wrong.

I haven't really had much to do with the elderly people of Newham, it was only when I went to the Homes. And if you want to talk about pain and suffering, you really wanna see what pain and suffering they went through when they were told their home's closing down, they weren't gonna see their friends. Ultimately, some of them died because of it. I was off sick for two weeks, I did take anti-depressants. But I'm sitting here talking about it. At least half a dozen elderly people died. And I think the main reason why they died, is because their Home closed. And they've got just as much right to live where they choose, as anyone else.

It's only then that I saw how elderly people have got no rights, really, in Newham, and young people haven't got any rights. If you're 18 to 45 in Newham, you're okay. If you're below that or you start going over, things are difficult. Nobody wants to employ people of 50. Anyone over 65 they stick in a Home. I can't believe there's people in homes in their 60s. I mean surely to God shouldn't put someone in to rot at 60-odd. I can't understand that. It's too late now. The Homes are all private now. And I think it's totally unfair for an elderly person's family to be required to give their savings because our borough can't be bothered to provide a service to look after people who have probably worked in this borough, regenerated money, labour, everything else in this borough.

One of the main attractions for me, for Helping Hands, it's not a kibbutz, but it's similar. When I first come here, everyone ate together, everyone worked more or less together. I mean everyone had different jobs, but – it was almost like a kibbutz, in a way. Without money. That's important for me.

I've never been very much money-orientated, although it's very important for me to provide for my family. I'm thankful, I've got a good job. But probably if I was single, I'd probably be quite happy to live somewhere like here, in a small, spartan room and be very very comfortable. But

Loading the van – ?!

Jivel at breakfast-time

obviously if you've got a family you can't think about things like that too much, though you might wish to.

The first time I came here, I was drinking a lot and I was going to see Dr Vellupuliae. He's a good old boy, he's a good doctor. And we had a chat for about half an hour, – it helped – but I kept on saying "I can't sleep," and what I really needed to say is "I'm drinking a lot, and I think I'm gonna crack up," to be honest. It was like a kick-back from Israel. I missed everything, and I wasn't happy. I was just unhappy with myself. And I always knew this place was here. So there was no flashing lights or a little star out there, I just knocked on the door. Cos I remembered the Brothers when I was a little boy, there was a Brother used to do magic, I used to follow him. Nicholas.

And it was Julian opened the door. Nearly 12 years ago. And I think I was here for about four hours, I just spewed it all out. I don't think I was religious then at all, I just needed to talk to someone. And I wanted to come here again. I just started coming here, sitting in reception. The Brothers were here then, it was a bit stricter, I think Alan was Julian's secretary, and I used to sit and joke with people in the drop-in. Get to know them.

And I enjoyed it. It was something good in my life. It was simple, I was with people who are not judgemental, they had their own problems which they shared, which to me was therapeutic in a way. I enjoyed their company. I started to participate more in what was happening here. Struck a good rapport with Julian. I think Julian's more than a good friend in a way, he's more like the older brother I've always wanted. I haven't got that many friends, and Julian is a true friend, but as a brother as well.

I'm very proud to be part of Helping Hands. It's in my blood. It's my retreat, it's my haven. The happiest I was, where I was the real Tom Nixon, was with my goats in the Negev. Well, this is almost on a level with that. I find great solitude and happiness here. I'm being very selfish there, but that's how I see it.

I don't get much time for myself, and I find this place my only retreat, where I can be me. If I didn't have this place I probably would have lost my identity a long time ago.

It's so easy to be lost in a world of make-belief, because that's all it is, all I do is pretend to be something I'm not. And I'm good at doing it. But I'm happy here. Really, really happy. I've met so many different people. I've seen everything, heard everything, smelt everything. I would recommend it to anyone, if they have the patience to sit and look closely at what really happens here. It's not just a house, it's a pulsating force where people who are ill, mentally and physically, can come and get better. Not completely. Because it never happens that way. But it's a place where you can be left alone to get better or get worse or whatever. You're left alone to do that, for a while. And I like that.

Some people don't realise what they can do here, they miss something, and it's not for them. Or they could abuse it. But it's a house that could be abused – it can take it, only so much, but I think it sympathises with abuse in a way. If it couldn't, the walls couldn't hold, they'd collapse. It's a strong house, a safe house.

I don't know what the future is gonna be. I've learnt not to plan now. I'd like to think, I'll be as old as John and I'll be sitting here moaning and whingeing, but in myown way help to keep Helping Hands going in our ideas. It's funny, my son Sean really likes it here. And I would never ever put him under any pressure, but I constantly look for someone or some people, who would be able to carry on.

Julian said it very well, Helping Hands is like the garden. You've got some flowers that come up every year, some that die and some that only come up for a day. But then you've got the trees which are there, solid, forever. And it's very difficult to find replacement trees, to grow quick enough. And if I'm worried, I'm not worried about the house closing down. Because you can never destroy an idea. You can destroy a house, but the way of Helping Hands I would hope would still be here. So that's what I try to identify with.

Coming home: back to where I belong. A dose of nostalgia hits me. I am flooded with memories. Some of them are pleasant and some of them are sad. Yet I can't stop smiling at the familiar sights I see. 'Has it really been this long?' I ask myself. Someone familiar approaches and with a big grin on my face I wave vigorously at him but he turns his face away and walks past me. I am shocked. I want to stop and query him. Surely he must remember me. After all, he is a face from my past. But on second thoughts I decide to let him go. Faces from the past can also be the faces of long-forgotten enemies.

I arrive at my house. It's still the same although it looks much smaller to me now. In those days it was such a noisy house and we never used the gate. So out of old habit I jump over the wall, half-expecting the old lady to come out of the house and scold me. But nothing happens. Silence. I stand my ground and finally the door opens andthe old lady comes out. But now she is bent, half blind.

'It's me,' I say to her. 'Is it really You?' she asks. 'Yes,' I reply.

We are both happy as we hug each other. I am also happy that at least one person remembers me. She quickly brings me up to date. Most of the girls are married now and the boys have all gone to the city in search of a better life. She no longer goes to church because it has been pulled down and a factory has been built in its place. The kids have all turned to crime, ever since the football field was turned into a rice farm. I am dumbfounded by her revelations.

After a while I am ready to move on. I say goodbye to her. Instead of replying, she demands to know my name. I shake my head in disbelief. Even she doesn't remember me. She is lonely and willing to talk to anyone. Even strangers. Everyone has moved on and I have become a stranger in my own home.

As I walk away, I know I will never come back here. But I am also amused at my stupidity. How on earth did I think that time would stand still and wait for the day I come home?

Izzy

6 *The silent ones*

The unspoken stories

One of the people of 42 is a hidden presence. Small and slight, he moves swiftly, light-footed. There is laughter in his voice. Unobtrusively, he is alert, aware, tuned in to what is happening around him. He is one of the hubs of the House, holding it in place. He told his story, then asked that it not be published.

He is not alone in asking for silence. As this book has taken shape, a shadowy group has gathered, gradually becoming more significant. Now, close to publication, it is no longer good enough merely to acknowledge these people in the foreword: they are part of the story, their silence eloquent.

For most contributors, there were questions of privacy, yet those who at last asked not to be included are with one exception members of ethnic minority groups. Their reasons are various. For two Muslims – from Pakistan and the Horn of Africa – family privacy was decisive. For a man born in Britain but with his upbringing and family in Nigeria, the issues were complex. Family privacy mattered a great deal, but almost more intractable was the question of how to express his story in a way that would not be misunderstood either here or back home in Nigeria. He was acutely aware of privilege in having access to a future in Britain; that must not be perceived as a rejection of his country. And there were other questions, yet trickier to handle. Silence was, he concluded, the only way; to publish would be to breed misunderstanding.

The ramifications of silence are endless. One refugee I wanted to ask but did not, knowing this book to be too blunt a tool. I have only heard him speak of his country when drunk; then, his words are lyrical, tumbling over each other, rarely making linear sense – a song of love for a lost land. Another, thinking of his family back home, could not take the risk of publication, even though he said nothing to criticise his government and even if we altered names and details.

It is easy for me, middle class westerner, to assume that it's good to talk, that to know more of each other is to understand more. "Sometimes", comes the answer. Silence is as valid as speech: each have their place. And knowledge of each other is not lightly gained. Fear of misunderstanding, and the desire to find words which say what was *really* meant, have marked several people's responses to reading their own transcript. Our experience has meaning in the context of our own culture and individual circumstances. Unless, somehow, we can convey that broader picture, to talk can worsen misconceptions. And communication demands effort also of the listener. "Why do these things, that to me have so little significance, matter so much to you?" Once ask that question and a lifetime of enquiry opens up, into worlds as subtle as they are complex and private, guarded against heavy-footed outsiders. Sometimes, the reasons for silence or the hesitations audible in the words raise questions about the speaker's world: what is the regime of fear, of guilt, or pride or grief which can so imprison this person? Sometimes they challenge the listener and her world: what am I, what kind of assumptions mould me, that this person should fear my response?

These stories are embedded in silence. The silence of those who have chosen not to speak and the silence of those who were not asked, whose stories will never be heard beyond their own circle, if there. The people whom we meet in these pages are a reminder of the always-hidden lives.

And silence is embedded in the stories. For everyone who spoke, there were no-go areas, either which they told then deleted from the text, or which they did not tell. Some people wanted to cut out as trivial some tiny incident or random image which they spoke almost without knowing it. Yet in those little things lies so much of the spirit of our lives: tiny gems, glimmering.

The story is never complete. But it acts as a signal, reminding us of the wholeness which cannot be told but which is there, often mutilated, misshapen by the muddles and cruelties of life, incomprehensible in its shapelessness; yet unique, speaking of the tenacity and hope that keep on living, day after day.

> The Tao that can be told is not the eternal Tao.
> The name that can be told is not the eternal name.
> The nameless is the beginning of heaven and earth.
> The named is the mother of ten thousand things.
>
> *Lao Tsu*

7 What's it all about?

A matter of respect – Donna's story

Donna is 20 and has a flat in Stratford. She came to Helping Hands as a New Deal trainee, staying on after her six months to help manage the trainees' work. Strongly built, she moves with a kind of slow, purposeful lope. She speaks fast and decisively, her infectious humour somehow underlining the seriousness of what she says.

I chose to come here. I was interested in caring, cos my mum was terminally ill and I looked after her like from a young age. So I was interested in care, and I still am, but not as I was before. Now I'd like to do an Access course, maybe go to university and be a social worker or do something like that. Whereas before, I was just willing to be like a support worker or a care assistant.

I've always wanted to go in the ambulance service as a care assistant. My mum used to get an ambulance to and fro the hospital, but I always bin interested in it before then. I think when it started was when I broke my leg, when I was nine. There was this guy, he was making jokes, and I mean my leg was broken in three places and my bone was sticking out my skin, and I was in agony, but he was still making me laugh and looking after me. So I'd like to be able to do that with disabled people and elderly people, just taking them to and fro the hospital. Wouldn't mean I'd be satisfied there. I wouldn't like to get to one point in my life and say this is where I wanna be. I'd always like to have something else to aim for. I've got plenty of time. Hopefully, in one order or the other, there'll be the ambulance service and university.

I've always thought about it, university, it's just that no one in my family before me has like finished school and gone off to college and done things like that. I mean, that's not looking down on them, cos I love them, but there's just never bin a role-model there. I suppose it'll be scarey, but it's what I want. And I always used to do what other people wanted me to do. And when you do things for other people, when it concerns yourself, I don't think it makes you strong enough to carry you all the way. So now, I know what I wanna do, it's something I want. I think if I was to do that, I would do pretty well.

I've got a little sister, so I'd like to give her a role-model, someone to look up to. She looks up to me already. She's smart, my little sister. But I'd like to do something so she can say "I wanna do this," or "I wanna do that." Because when I was making that decision, when I was leaving school, I found it very hard. I applied to ten colleges and I got accepted to all ten, so I had all the options there, but I still found it hard. Because no one in front of me had done it. So it was pretty scarey, cos I was gonna be the one doing it myself. And I remember like people feeling funny cos I'd gone that distance, and they thought that I thought I was better than them. Which is not true at all, because everyone goes their own different ways, and no matter what they do, I still have a great deal of respect for them. It's just that I don't wanna go down that road, I prefer to go down another one.

Being at Helping Hands has gave me a lot of respect. Because I think when people respect you and you haven't got a lot of respect for yourself, it makes you look at yourself and think well, why are they respecting me? So you have to kind of look at yourself, look at the good points rather than sometimes, people focus on their own bad points. I mean, I joke around with people and muck around, and I've always done that from the beginning, but I've never really recognised the capability that I have, and if somebody said I had that capability I might have made a joke out of it, where I didn't wanna see it. Cos you have to act on it, don't you, and it's a scarey prospect. Yeah, exciting. But scarey.

I mean everything's scarey, but once you get past that... I was worried about spending six months here. The first week was hard. Very hard. Not because of the people, but because of myself. I wasn't comfortable in myself, so I made myself feel uncomfortable. I thought no, I'm not coming back. Then I was thinking right, I'm gonna go back. So why am I gonna go back? I'm gonna go back because I'm gonna get this experience, get an NVQ and then I'm gonna get a job and blablabla. So I had to look at it like that. I had to look down the road, I had to jump over what I was scared of and look down the road to see, like this is the only way I can get there. Like blackmail myself into it.

And I took two weeks off, and then when I come back, I come back thinking differently. I don't know why, but I just felt more confident. Cos I wasn't so new, I just felt more comfortable. So then I started noticing things like the job book, wanting to know about that. And then asking Julian how the jobs got booked and things like that. Just inquisitive. And then I'd bin here about five months, Julian said to me about some jobs that had come in, he said to me about I know the people better, and see who's best for the jobs and that. So I was happy with that, because it's something new that I've learnt.

I didn't know at the beginning that I would end up doing the role I am. But I am glad, because I've now found that I am more suited to this. Because I am like naturally an organised person. If you look in my wardrobe, it's all organised, if you go in my bathroom, the toothpaste has got the roll at the bottom! It can be aggravating sometimes, I've bin told. But I just assumed that I'd be better in the role of care, because I've done it before. Because when it's like your mum, it's natural, but when it's other people, I feel quite uncomfortable sometimes. So I am better suited to what I'm doing now.

I have in a way seen myself as a leader, but not so much in a work environment. All through school, all the sports teams I was in, I was captain of. And then I was student counsellor, and first I was class representative and then year representative and then school representative in discussions and stuff, so it's always bin there, but I've never really recognised it. I think it's inside everybody, but it takes a certain thing for them to question themselves and notice it. And some people notice it and then go over the top, and then people think they're obnoxious! Hopefully I won't go that far.

Coming here does open your eyes, cos there's so many different people here. If you come with certain views and then you meet someone and you get to know them, then the views that you've got, you've got to question them because they was presumptions, they weren't truths. Now you've got the truth in front of you so you've got to question yourself. I haven't had to do that too much, cos where I was brought up with my mum, I was never racist against black people, because I am half black. Although I could have bin, because of what happened, but then I could have bin racist against white people cos my mum's family turned against her. But I was just open about most things. So I think it's just immaturity when you look at someone and you think they're weird, you presume things.

Where I was before, the people I was meeting was through my choice. But here, you don't have the choice of who you meet. Cos you can't say, "I'll talk to you, but I won't talk to you." I wouldn't like it done to me, and I wouldn't do it. But if you go through life you have a choice who you want to talk to and who you want to meet. You can meet people, but if you don't want to know them or talk to them it's pretty easy to get away from them. Here, you can't do that.

I study personalities and things like that, it just interests me. Just the way they think. I mean like Jason and Garry, the way their minds work, it just amazes me, and because of that I've got a lot of respect for them. And Kenny, Kenny's sense of humour. And Rose, Rose is complex, but you can't help just liking her.

I remember Julian coming to my house to see my mum, I was about 16. And I thought he was weird. I really thought he was weird. I remember him knocking on the door, and I wasn't sure whether I should like say "no thanks," and shut the door in his face, like a Jehovah's Witness or something. And I shut the door, and I said to my mum, "Mum, there's some man at the door, he's got a brown sack thing on, with a rope." And she said to me, "open the door, it's Brother Julian." So I opened it, and I apologised and everything. But it's just like, when you see people from the outside, you don't know nothing and you presume. But when you get to know them, you see a different side. Like when I come in the first day, it felt a bit weird, being in a room with some weird people. But you just get to know people and understand. And I think people have certain views of things, but they're not really educated about it. They didn't know at first that I was gay, I've never hid it, but I've never openly said it. But everybody knows now, nobody treats me differently or in a funny way because of it.

If you lie about a thing in the beginning and then you come out about it afterwards, that can tend to cause a bit of upset. But I've never done that, because as far as I'm concerned I am who I am, and if people don't like it, it's tough really. They ain't gotta like it. Because my mum married a black man, her family didn't like it, so they disowned her. So my mum just taught me to be who I wanna be, and if people don't like that, it's their problem. I always learned that, if somebody didn't like the way I am or who I am, it's their loss.

Frank and Albert

I don't see the point in lying about anything. I don't like lies, so I don't tell them. It doesn't mean I walked in here on my first day and said, "this is who I am," did a dance, performed! But as you get to know people they ask you certain questions – I mean, I remember Daphne asking me if I had a young man, so rather than saying "oh yes," blablabla, I just said at the time I wasn't with anybody, but if I was with anybody it would be a woman, because I'm gay. And I think there was a bit of an atmosphere at first, not with Daphne, but as more and more people were finding out, they were sort of like questioning themselves, and it was sort of understandable. And it was all right after that. I had a couple of people ask me questions, and it wasn't a problem cos I'd rather people ask me questions and I answer and they find out the truth, rather than them presuming. I mean, it's just about educating people. If I can do that, fair enough. Because if I don't understand about somebody, I'll ask questions as well. And I have done. I have asked people questions.

I remember when I was younger, I didn't like to meet people and talk to people. But now it's the opposite, the complete opposite. I dunno, I think I had a portion of chips on me shoulder or something! Now I've just got a few! I think you look at it differently when you're younger. It's easy to feel sorry for yourself, and look at everything, and look at other people, and see them with their mum and their dad and their family around them and things like that. It's easy to feel sorry for yourself, like when they've got a new mountain bike and you haven't or something. But when you get older, it just makes you value the people you have got.

It's easy to get bitter. It's destructive, it's destroying yourself. I can sit there and moan about what's happened, and say "oh feel sorry for me feel sorry for me". I could have bin that sort of person, and I probably was just after my mum died. But when you're that way, it's like you're only hurting yourself, it's not only other people hurt you, it's your past hurting you and people you meet can hurt you, and you're hurting yourself. That way, you can only lose. And I've never bin interested in losing too much. Not that I wanna win anything, but I'd like to be able to achieve something.

As long as I respect myself, it doesn't really bother me what others think. If I'm behaving in a certain way and it's not right, then I'll know it myself, and I'll punish myself for it. The person I am, I try not to behave in that way, but it does happen sometimes. But when it does happen, you've just got to do your best to make the situation good again. From a young age, my mum's taught me to have respect for myself. If we did something wrong, she didn't hit us or shout and scream or anything. I don't know what it was. It was just it automatically felt bad, so when I did something, I felt bad. I don't know how she done it. Because when I done something wrong, I was worried about telling my mum but I knew like I had to tell her, because otherwise I'd feel bad for ages and ages.

And somebody I respected a lot, she sat me down and made me look at certain things in myself, and look at other people, and see how I am different. I don't think I would've, if my mum had still lived. I wouldn't have had to question myself. It's really hard to do, but sometimes you come to a point where you have to do it, otherwise you just gonna self-destruct. So I had to choose between recognising myself, recognising my abilities, or self-destruct. A choice. I mean, you feel the pain and hurt and things like that, but then you've gotta make certain decisions about yourself.

I never feel alone. I don't believe I've lost out on anything. I think if anything I've gained. Although my family was very racist, because it was like a stigma to have a daughter who was married to a black man and have his children. People say like you can't choose your family, but I do. When I meet someone and I class them that close, then they're family. Because some people with their families, it's like a duty. If they have to choose between spending time with their brother, or with their friend, they'd rather spend time with their friend, but it's their duty to spend time with their brother. And I've never really fancied that myself.

I've met a lot of people that I've talked to and been friends with them, but there's not a lot of people that I would like hold close to me. Because the way that I look upon someone, and respect them and care about them, would be more than they would about me. Not because I'm better than them, but it's the way that they're looking at themselves. Where they're not completely satisfied with themselves, they're not capable to give out certain things. When I meet people, just through the way I treat them, they get more respect about themselves. That's not many people. It's not to say that I don't class them as friends, cos I do. I have got respect for everyone in that room, and everyone who would sit in that room in the past or in the future, and I would help them in any way I could. But there's people who I naturally like click with and feel closer to and talk to in more detail about things.

Race, I don't think it's too much of an issue here. It is for one or two, but they're not brave enough to stand up and let it known. Because even now, if you see somebody walking down the road and it's a black man and a white woman, people still give you funny looks. But it's not just white people giving them funny looks, it's black people as well. Cos when you're mixed race, you get a lot of aggro from white people and black people. If somebody's gonna have an argument with you, the first thing that's gonna come out their mouth is, like if they're white then you're black, if they're black then you're white, or if you're neither then you're a mongrel, something like that.

I had it here. It was on my birthday. I don't know the guy's name, I've seen him a couple of times. And he was ringing on the doorbell, and Julian was telling me about a job. And it was important, it was about a client, so I needed to know. So I put my hand up, to say "yeah, I know you're there, I'll get the door in a second." And he kept ringing, so I said to Julian, "I'll just get the door." And I went to the door and I opened it, and he went, "about time, you fucking nigger." And I wasn't very pleased. And he kept going off about "you fat wog" and all this, and then he went, "if I was a fucking woman," he went, "I bet you'd have opened the door faster, you fat lesbian." I find that rather amusing. Because he was in this house and I've got respect, I didn't do nothing, but if I was out on the street, I would have done something about it.

But things like that don't really bother me, because it just shows me how pathetic that person is. Rather than taking it to heart or anything, it don't bother me. Because I give everybody respect, because that's what I've learnt. They don't have to earn it in my eyes, but then if they do something or say something I don't like, that's when they lose the respect I give them. So if I had a lot of respect for someone, like Garry or someone, and he said it, then that would hurt, but apart from that, doesn't really bother me.

I think if you're comfortable in a place, then it won't happen so much, because you won't be so worried about what you gotta say. If you're more comfortable, more relaxed, then you seem to be more relaxed with people, and people seem to be more relaxed with you. Because if you allow people to walk all over you, then they're gonna do it, but if you're just there and you're just like "this is who I am, if you don't like it, you

John the Buddhist

don't have to," then I think you'll get more respect than if you try to please everybody. Because once you start that, you're doing it for the rest of your life, running around after people. And you don't get no respect for running around after people.

The Job Centre, they was going to send me to a nursing home. But I said no, it's not the environment I want. Because I know that there's a lot of abuse that goes on in institutions, whether it's nursing homes, hospitals, prisons, anywhere. And I can't see that. I'm the sort of person, if someone's having trouble in the street, like a man hitting a woman or a woman hitting a kid, then I'd say something. Because in my eyes, it shouldn't happen. Whatever's the reasons, it shouldn't happen.

I've seen it before. There's a club opposite my house, and there was these two, I think they was two gay girls, and one of them was really butch, she was huge, and she was beating up this little woman. And I didn't interfere because I'm gay and I think it's my duty, I interfered because it was somebody harming someone else. And I was well upset – I had this white Gap jean suit on, I was only 16. And everyone was standing around and watching and not doing nothing. I sort of like had to break my way through this crowd, and she chucked a punch and I sort of like stood away, I picked up the little one and started to walk away with her. And she started swearing at me, and even *she* called me a black cunt and things like that, so it happens everywhere. She come behind me and grabbed me behind the throat and everything. So I put the little one down, and I just said to some guy who was standing there, I said to him, "look after her." I'm getting dragged back by my throat, so I turned round and pushed her off me and said, "look I'm not interested in fighting you, but I'm not gonna stand around and let you hurt someone like that." She said, "it's none of your business" blablabla. I said, "fair enough, I'm making it my business." I said, "you're just like disrespecting yourself, making yourself look stupid." She was hellbound on having a fight, so I let her chuck a couple of slaps till she was satisfied, then I hit her and she fell down, and I left it.

But as I was walking away there was someone said, "you shouldn't have got involved" blablabla. And I just started screaming my head off, I felt like I was preaching, because there was like 40 people, they were standing around doing nothing, and I was saying like "haven't you got no respect for yourself," blablabla. And after I finished what I was saying, I felt quite bad, but I hope that what I said made them think, so if there was a fight another time, they would stop it or something. I don't like getting angry, I don't like shouting or being aggressive or something like that. When I am, because it's something I don't like about myself, I feel bad. But hopefully, something good come out of it.

I've always liked – not arguing as such, but putting forward a point and arguing my point. Although I accept other people's points. Cos me and Charmaine have arguments all the time, because she calls herself half-caste and I won't call myself half-caste, even if I was strapped down and whipped like 20 times, I wouldn't call myself half-caste. Like I think lesbian sounds – it's not a nice word. I don't like it. You get gay men, gay means happy, you get lesbian, it's just an ugly word, I've never liked it. I won't call myself a lesbian.

I don't like to put myself in categories. Sometimes you have to, but then when you box yourself, there's stereotypes that come along with the box. And I don't like fitting into stereotypes. So that's it.

Looking to the future – Julian's story

Julian, medium-tall and thinly-built, is never seen to rush. His hallmarks are his slow, smooth steps and slow, calm-sounding voice – and his laugh, that echoes through the house and street. He's 41, a Brother since 1979, in Balaam Street for 16 years.

At the end of each day, it is reported that St Francis, the little poor man of Assisi, turned to his companion and said, "Brother Leo, let us begin again, for until now we have done nothing."

This "beginning again" is a practical imperative on the path of obedience, that attentive listening to the voice of the present moment, making new our loving response in each unfolding situation. It is a way of life in which we take nothing for granted, divest ourselves of assumptions and are surprised by the wonders being created for us, in us, by us. It is a letting go into the unknowable future.

A gift of the local Buddhist temple

Descending from Mount Alvena, a wild crag in Umbria, Brother Leo, anxious for their safety, turned to St Francis and asked, "Brother Francis, where is the way?" And Francis replied, "Brother Leo, there is no way. Leap!" Such drama is, perhaps, not our everyday experience. Certainly we do not expect a saint as a companion. Yet in our common home, 42 Balaam Street, the little poor man of Assisi is pleased to dwell, nudging us from time to time to start again and take a leap into the unknown.

Reading our story, individual and collective, St Francis is delighting in the bubbling up of his spirit. When "worker" John says, "done things that's gotta be done, and that's it," he takes us to the practical essence of Francis' poverty, that givenness to life, with no rights and no fuss, just doing the next thing. Sometimes John worries that he does the wrong thing. Here, Garry helps us to leap. He says, "I want to be wrong for ever. Do you understand that? I want to have somebody say well you're wrong there, and I go, oh, that's a good point. And I can develop it. I never want that to stop. Just seeing beauty. Discovering beauty like language."

Our future, as we grow in faithfulness, will be to see beauty. The joy of the East End is to discover that beauty in unexpected, hidden places. St Francis is renowned for his love of nature, surrounded by animals, preaching to birds. In art and popular imagination, he has become a rather sentimental figure, far removed from the struggle for survival which preoccupies most of us.

Yet allow St Francis to begin to tell us his story. He wrote his *Testament* shortly before his death in 1226. He begins by revealing "how God inspired me, Brother Francis, to embark upon a life of penance." As a young man, Francis had enjoyed wealth, prestige and many privileges. He was a fun-loving, party-going reveller. He lived in a sharply divided society. The lowest stratum, lepers, were excluded completely. The sight and stench of a leprosy sufferer nauseated the young Francis: he was a person of his age, never wholly free, as none of us ever are, of the assumptions in which he had grown up.

One day, riding outside Assisi, the horse bearing Francis reared up, startled by a movement in the ditch beside the road. Looking down, Francis beheld rotting flesh and fearful eyes. He reached for his purse, pulled out a few coins, threw them at the leper and rode on. It was a response which he would have made many times before.

Then, he did something completely different. He turned his horse, rode back to the mysterious figure, dismounted and embraced the rotting flesh. At that moment, Francis began to discover the strength of his life. What had previously nauseated him became the very meaning and motivation of his being. In the leper, Francis found his life. In the leper, Francis saw beauty.

This is the starting point for us all to root our vision in the ditch beside the road where we, our brothers and our sisters are at risk of being trampled underfoot by the powerful, rich and proud. Each of us has our core of vulnerability, our secret agony, our shameful darkness. We are brothers and sisters who, in our poverty, have everything to give to each other: the very meaning of our lives.

To paraphrase the writings of Mgr Leonidas Proano, Bishop of Riobamba,

To feel as our own the suffering
Of a brother, sister, near or far,
To make our own the anguish of the poor.
That is solidarity.

To let ourselves be transported by a message
Charged with hope, love and peace,
Until we clasp our brothers, sisters, by the hand.
That is solidarity.

Kofi Annan, Secretary-General of the United Nations, writes that "When I talk of the United Nations I am not talking only of the staff, and those occupying our offices; I am talking of the United Nations of 'We the peoples' [the opening words of the UN Charter]. When we all pull together from across the world and work together to solve a problem, we almost always can do it." He continued, with emotion, "Never underestimate the power of prayer."

Rooting our vision in the ditch beside the road, let it grow to embrace every strange, unfamiliar, uncomfortable situation which we encounter. Let us join hands with friends whom we did not know, and draw close to brothers and sisters whom we thought alien. Let us, in the vision of Old John's story, "marry the world."

Looking to the future... Old John reminds me of St Francis when he says, "I didn't know the first thing about loving the body." Francis, so open to beauty around him, neglected to look after his own body; in a sense, he failed to appreciate the beauty in that most unexpected of places, himself.

Maybe, as Francis grew older, he would echo Old John again: "the older I get, I look around. Like you and I talking, amazing that there's vibration, there's a link! I mean, the wonder of the world, looking at the flower, the beauty, the sound, and having the faculties to see beauty and that in simple little things... we don't give ourselves time to enjoy the moment. We want to fetch the next."

In the words of St Francis, Peace, and every good, to each one of us.

Piotr, Idris, Joshua and Julian in the garden

8 Postscript

Big Alan

with thanks for the grace of God

Alan's left us. Big Alan, gentle Alan, mountain of a man, has died. He had a bug, some kind of 'flu', we thought; nothing much, save that Alan's never ill. Then intensive care, in a coma. 'He's fighting back,' his friend told us; he could squeeze her hand. Then he died.

Big Alan, gentle giant – how can we mourn you, what can we say of you? Big and square, slow-moving, inarticulate. Craggy face, revealing little till it cracked into a smile, warm as the fire on the hearth; with a twinkle of mischief, unexpected. Alan saw more than he said, remembered what he needed; let the rest go.

Always here. Doorbell rings, Alan on the doorstep, grunting good morning. Sits down, hands square on thighs; grey-haired, ageless. Then he and John, little John, small and wiry, collect their tools and jobsheets: off they go, big Al and small John bobbing beside him, up to Upton Park, down to Canning Town, round to East Ham, tools over their shoulders; knock at the door, listen to what's needed: size up the job and get on with it – trimming the hedge, strimming the lawn, shifting the rubbish into the dustbin sacks. And the extra jobs which mysteriously appear at the last moment. Could they just – shift the double bed downstairs, move the wardrobe, clear that rubbish... They're never paid; all they have is the basics for life, but the people they work for need them – old or infirm; lonely; anxious. Alan and John are part of the scene, one of the certainties in a stress-filled world. On a removal, it's Alan who stands and considers the truculent, bulgy three-piece, coaxes it through the door and round the angle – or, once, through the window. It's Alan who persuades the heart-sinking medley of furniture to relax its knobbly intransigence and cuddle down together in the van so there's room for all. Big Alan, gentle Alan, strong mountain of a man.

Alan was indestructible; always there. Alan cared. That's why we needed him – so many hidden lives in Plaistow, East Ham, Upton Park and Canning Town all needed him: big Alan, mountain of a man. Why we need his memory, as a earnest of what's real and indestructible.

Buffeted by life three centuries ago, an early Quaker found that "hope underneath held me, as an anchor in the bottom of the sea", so his soul could "swim above the raging waves, foul weather, tempest...". Alan anchored us, holding us firmly to what is good and strong and indestructible in human life. Thank you.

Old John